ANGEL ABUNDANCE

"In their new book, the 12 Archangels make it clear that to solve the problems we face as human beings we must transform our own heartache, both known to us as well as what is hidden in the deep subconscious. In this practical guide, channeled at the pure frequency of love, the Angels show us the way to free ourselves, and the collective, from lack and suffering. It begins with connecting with Source through the feminine so that we rise from limitations imposed on us by the old male patriarchy. Bravo, Belinda and the Angels, for revealing the truth about money and lighting the path to real abundance."

REGINA MEREDITH, HOST OF *OPEN MINDS* ON GAIA TV

"*Angel Abundance* is mesmerizing. Written with the wisdom that comes from facing real-life financial challenges, it inspires the reader to truly know and feel our connection with God and the Angels. Abundance is our birthright. This book will guide you to that reality."

CHRISTIANE NORTHRUP, M.D., NEW YORK TIMES
BESTSELLING AUTHOR OF *GODDESSES NEVER AGE*

"Belinda and the 12 Archangels' work in this book is profound, to say the least. *Angel Abundance* is a guiding light for all those souls who want to connect to inner wealth in this age of massive awakening around the world."

ALEX FERRARI, HOST OF THE *NEXT LEVEL SOUL* PODCAST

ANGEL ABUNDANCE

REVELATIONS ON TRUE WEALTH
FROM THE 12 ARCHANGELS

Belinda J. Womack

Bear & Company
Rochester, Vermont

Bear & Company
One Park Street
Rochester, Vermont 05767
www.BearandCompanyBooks.com

Text stock is SFI certified

Bear & Company is a division of Inner Traditions International

Cataloging-in-Publication Data for this title is available from the Library of Congress

ISBN 978-1-59143-498-6 (print)
ISBN 978-1-59143-499-3 (ebook)

Printed and bound in the United States by Lake Book Manufacturing, LLC
The text stock is SFI certified. The Sustainable Forestry Initiative® program
promotes sustainable forest management.

10 9 8 7 6 5 4 3 2

Text design and layout by Kenleigh Manseau
This book was typeset in Garamond Premier Pro with Bookmania and Gotham
used as display typefaces

To send correspondence to the author of this book, mail a first-class letter to the
author c/o Inner Traditions • Bear & Company, One Park Street, Rochester, VT
05767, and we will forward the communication, or contact the author directly at
www.BelindaWomack.com.

For Michael, twin of my Soul,
and our pets who care for us,
Bella, Galaxy, and Grace

❖❖❖

Contents

Preface: Living in Abundance
with the 12 Archangels   xiii

PART I

Accepting the Invitation

The Invitation   2
   ❀ *Receiving the Invitation*   5

Spiritual Laws That Help You   7
   ❀ *A New Beginning*   15

PART 2

Raising Your Vibration

Definition of Wealth   18

The Singing Colors of the Central Sun   21
   ❀ *Rainbow Embrace*   26

The Purple Door   28
   ❀ *Stepping through the Purple Door*   30
   ❀ *Restoring in the Energy Fountains*   32

Keeping Watch for the Old
Male and the Old Female   35
⚚ *Love Alarm*   39

The Healing Gifts of the Divine
Inner Child   41
⚚ *Receiving Guidance and Healing*   43

Changing the Repetitive
Story of Lack   45
⚚ *Transforming Subconscious
    Unworthiness and Guilt*   47
⚚ *Healing the Wounded Self*   50
⚚ *Transmuting Lack Beliefs*   56
⚚ *Releasing Ancestral and Past-Life Trauma*   58

PART 3

Receiving Your Wealth

What Does Wealth Look Like to You?   60
⚚ *Releasing the Expectation of
    Being Abandoned by Creator*   62
⚚ *Filling Up with All You Could Ever Want*   63
⚚ *Freedom Within, Freedom Without*   64
⚚ *Undiluted Love for You*   65
⚚ *Doubt Out, Trust In*   67

The Twin Sisters of Intuition
and Creativity   68
⚚ *Releasing the Negative Parent Voice*   71
⚚ *Letting Go of the Magic Parent*   75

Your Creativity Garden   76
⚚ *Preparation: Clearing Repression of
    the Feminine*   76
⚚ *Planting Your Creativity Garden*   79
⚚ *Germination: Freeing the
    Repressed Masculine*   80

⚘ *Playing in the Garden of Your
Creative Imagination*   82
⚘ *Firing Up Your Creativity*   85

Cultivating with Heart Power   89
⚘ *Transforming Your Heartache*   91
⚘ *Activating Heart Power*   96

Harvesting Your Garden   98
⚘ *Rescuing the Ego*   100

PART 4

Creating a New Financial Reality

The Divine Laws and Money   104
⚘ *Clearing Financial Trauma and Suffering*   107

Transforming the Fear Held within
the Thoughtform of Money   110
⚘ *Releasing the Puppet Strings of
Attachment to Money*   114

Dissolving Financial Debt with
Understanding and Love   116
⚘ *Conquering Doubt*   118
⚘ *Credit and Validation for You*   122
⚘ *Transforming Family Patterns of Debt*   124

Creativity and Sustainable Flow   127
⚘ *Clearing the Pipeline*   131
⚘ *Receive, Attract, Focus, and Grow!*   132

PART 5

What Is Still Missing?

The 12 Archangels' Formula to Change
Your Reality   138

To Love and Be Loved   142
  ❀ *Forgiving the Past*   *146*

The Freedom to Choose   148
  ❀ *Transforming Fear Caused by Religion*
     and Government   *151*

Living the Mission of Your Soul   153
  ❀ *Entering the Sanctuary of Soul*   *156*

Mental, Emotional, and Physical Health   158
  ❀ *Healing Session with the Angel Physicians*   *161*
  ❀ *Graceful Exit from the Dance Floor*   *162*

Peace and Balance: So Within,
So Without   164
  ❀ *Bringing Peace and Balance to Earth*   *165*

PART 6

Moving Schoolroom Earth
Out of Suffering

Transforming Poverty   170
  ❀ *Letting Go of Fear's Old Female*
     Poverty Beliefs   *171*
  ❀ *Transforming Poverty from the Inside Out*   *172*

Transforming Exile and Homelessness   175
  ❀ *Violet Fire for Releasing the Trauma of Exile*   *176*

Transforming Neglect and Abuse
of Children   178
  ❀ *Forgiving the Traumas of Childhood*   *182*
  ❀ *DNA Scrub for Clearing Neglect and Abuse*   *183*

Transforming Hatred, Violence,
and Evil with Undiluted Love   186
  ❀ *Divine Rescue*   *187*

Transforming Inequality,
Racism, and Discrimination   189
  🏵 *Transmuting the Judges*   *191*

Transforming Leadership and
the Misuse of Power   193
  🏵 *Reclaiming Your Highest Vibrational Will*   *195*

Transforming the Games of
Warfare and Military Action   197
  🏵 *Working with the Young Masculine*   *199*
  🏵 *Transforming or Eliminating Conflict*
    from the Inside Out   *201*

Transforming the Patriarchal Hierarchy   203
  🏵 *Deep Cleansing for the*
    Old Male and Old Female   *205*

Transforming Pollution and the
Exploitation of Natural Resources   207
  🏵 *Rebalancing the Power of the Divine Feminine*   *212*

Transforming Fear into Love   214
  🏵 *Healing the Divine Inner Child*   *215*

PART 7

Healing Experiences to Support
Restful Sleep and Happy Receiving

🏵 *Goodbye Negativity and Good Night!*   *219*
🏵 *Dragon's Roost with the Divine Inner Child*   *220*
🏵 *Divine Mothers' Palace of Renewal*   *221*
🏵 *Surfing with the 12 Archangels*   *222*
🏵 *Merlin's Cabin and Cocoa*   *223*
🏵 *Into the Purple Sea*   *225*
🏵 *Emerald and Ruby in a Golden Nest Egg*   *227*
🏵 *Mother Earth's Haven*   *228*
🏵 *Gratitude for You*   *230*

✤ *Emerald Forest*   *231*
✤ *Orchard of Ever-Growing Currency Trees*   *233*
✤ *Golden Pyramid of Initiation with*
  the 12 Archangels   *235*

◈◈◈

Acknowledgments   237

The 12 Archangels' Glossary of Terms   238

Index   249

ℒiving in ℵbundance with the 12 Archangels

Living in abundance with the 12 Archangels of the Central Sun started while I was struggling with a lack of money and a lack of self-confidence. Let's go back some thirty years when I was invited to a Meet Your Guardian Angels workshop. Months prior to the workshop, I had a surprise visit from Archangel Gabriel that turned my life upside down. Gabriel told me that I was soon to leave my job as a pediatric cancer research technician to help human beings reconnect with their divinity. I was completely confused. Everything I believed I knew and worked so hard to attain was dissolving before my eyes. By attending the workshop, I was hoping to gain some understanding of what was happening to me.

The teacher of the class guided us into meditation. We were told it may take a full ninety minutes to meet our two Angels. My head was splitting. I was not a meditator; I was a biologist. What on *earth* was I doing in this class? I closed my eyes and connected with my inner child. Somehow I knew to focus my mind on sensing her presence. She helped me to ignore the distraction coming from the fierce pain in the middle of my head that much later I learned was the reawakening of inner sight. "Little Belinda," as I call her, took me by the hand, and we stepped into a circle of colorful lights. At first all I could see was swirling color and then I saw them: 12 huge Angels, each holding a gift. I immediately had the thought that I had done something wrong because I was supposed to connect with two Angels, not 12. I remember Gabriel stepping into the circle and giving the gift of communication. Michael was next with the gift of Truth at the highest vibration of love. I do not remember the other ten gifts given that day, but I trust my Little Belinda received them for me and that we have used them and shared them for decades.

A few months after meeting the 12 Archangels of the Central Sun I left my job and, shortly after that, it dawned on me that I was in big trouble. I had no savings, no employment, and a mortgage loan heading to foreclosure. I was drowning in panic. To be completely honest, I had this ungrounded and completely crazy idea that when you work for God, money magically appears in your bank account. In desperation, I asked the Angels, who I assumed knew nothing about working for a living, what I was supposed to do to earn mine. I found out that they had been waiting for me to ask. The Angels swiftly made it apparent that they know a lot about helping humans with financial resources, especially when they are called to work in spiritual service. I was instructed to sit down at my computer and compose the messages transmitted to me. Surrendering to being a channel was my first step. My second step was to teach a class to a small group of kind and patient spiritual friends using the guidance I had received. Each student paid twenty-five dollars, and every penny was a miracle!

The day after the workshop, one of the participants asked me a question about her manufacturing-machinery sales business. Mind you, I knew nothing about manufacturing machinery, but out of my mouth came the words, "I can help you. Would you like a session with the 12 Archangels and your Guides?"

In those days, there were no such things as websites, social media, or internet marketing and yet, one client after another would arrive at my door. The Angels taught me to practice trust in Source, along with how to change my financial reality from the inside out. I had to believe in myself as a conduit for their love and straightforward honesty, and they needed to fill me with faith in myself. I learned that the ego cannot give to self what the ego does not have in the first place. We must ask Mother-Father-God and Soul (the higher Self) to give us what is missing, and, in my case, this was a sense of self-worth.

For more than thirty years, I have continued to live—and share with others—this insight from the Angels. For those who are brave and willing to surrender fully to their Soul's vocation, undiluted love is the wealth, flowing from Source, that converts into financial resources on the material plane. I have witnessed that as one's reliance on Soul deepens, the ego's control lessens and real and lasting abundance grows.

It is essential that we keep our vibration as clear and loving as possible throughout the day to help the ego let go of fear and control. For this reason, when I record the Angels' messages, they make sure that I use words that vibrationally transmit the Truth and nothing less. Whether I am communicating their teaching through writing or speaking, I monitor my vibration and stay grounded in undiluted love. This is especially the case when translating the energy of the Angels into written text. During the editing process of *Angel Abundance,* I would ask the Angels to confirm the vibrational frequency of the edits made by my kind and brilliant agent, Jane Lahr.

To help the reader experience a positive shift in vibration and feel the energy, we purposefully capitalize certain words such as *Angel, Truth, Heart,* and *Soul.* As your eyes pay attention to the capital letter at the beginning of the word, your feminine intuitive brain knows to raise the frequency from that of Earth to that of Heaven! Let me give you an example of how this works. Do you feel the vibrational difference when seeing the words *angel* and *Angel* or *divine oneness* and *Divine Oneness*? For a similar reason, the Angels provide you with a glossary of terms to help you feel the Truth in the rich teachings of *Angel Abundance.* Feel free to wander into the garden of the glossary and experience the healing love planted there. Always take your divine inner child with you because this Child is the key that opens the vault to the greatest riches of Creator. My Little Belinda proves this to me every day.

The 12 Archangels ask us to live within Heart, a vibration of undiluted love that is powerful and life changing. From this sanctuary of Heaven within us, we can receive all that we desire that provides us with real happiness. They encourage us to do this by lifting our low-vibration thoughts, feelings, perceptions, and expectations out of fear and into Trust. Living in abundance with Angels is the best way to create a never-ending, happy childhood where we feel secure, valued, and free. May you, too, uncover your authentic Self and discover the creative genius that is yours. As you exchange your vast riches with others, it is divine law that prosperity will flow to you. The 12 Archangels look forward to guiding *you* in the accelerated discovery of your true wealth.

ENJOY THE ADVENTURE!
BELINDA

PART I

Accepting the Invitation

*We invite you to use Soul's singing light to receive your
wealth from the Great Universe.*

THE 12 ARCHANGELS OF THE CENTRAL SUN

The Invitation

We are the 12 Archangels of the Central Sun, Soul of Source. We are infinitely loving forces of positive change, and our Souls are excited to send healing from the Central Sun to you. The Central Sun is composed of the energy we call love. Love energy is creative and expansive. The energy of undiluted love is Source, the energy that is God and the energy that is Creator of all. Love is the greatest and strongest alchemical power that exists anywhere in the Great Universe, including your fascinating blue planet we call "Schoolroom Earth."

As the codesigners of Schoolroom Earth, we want humanity to know that we cherish Archangel Gaia. Together with Creator, we infuse our undiluted love with each breath she gives to you. Gaia, planet Earth, is a destination where you are given the opportunity to experience the infinite dilutions of love energy known as fear. With each incarnation, you receive our invitation to use the singing rays of the Central Sun to transform the fear that makes you doubt your true worth and your phenomenal creative ability. We desire to help you let go of the many layers of doubt and fear that pull you into a vibrational reality that the human collective has outgrown. You have always had the ability to receive directly from Creator, and you have the power within you to move humanity from lack to abundance.

We will use the Power of undiluted love to help you feel and know that you are God's divine Child, equal in quality to an Archangel and eternally worthy of experiencing abundance. You too are a divine being and your Soul, like our Souls, ultimately originated from the One Soul. You may want to know our names; we have many, some understood and some misunderstood by your beautiful egos. Instead of distracting you with names and titles, we ask that you know us by our love and friendship. Why are we a team of 12? Our number is metaphoric and symbolizes the cycles of evolution moving humanity upward in vibration with each revolution of the sacred spiral of Creator's energy. Twelve is a number that fuses Sound and Light together to create Heart Power, the force that holds all Souls together in Divine Oneness. Our Sound moves your emotions, and our Light lifts the frequency of your thoughts. As you connect with our Sound and Light through our words, know that the language used in this text is purposefully designed to illuminate fear's seductive ways that want to put you back to sleep. We need you to be awake and to free the spiritual, creative, and emotional intelligence locked within your feminine intuitive brain.

Let us explain to you how Schoolroom Earth works. You, like Creator, create your positive reality (happy experiences) with love expressed through what you believe, think, and feel. Unlike Creator, you create the lack and disappointment in your life from fear-saturated beliefs primarily housed in your subconscious. You may have inherited these low vibration beliefs, brought them into this life from past lives to transform them, or agreed to take them on for the One Human Body (collective). In each incarnation, you agree to transform suffering through your own personal transformation and ascension (breaking free of limitation).

Humanity's deepest and most harmful subconscious fears are that Mother-Father-God has abandoned you to survive on a dangerous and unfair planet and that you will be punished if you ask for help from God. Intimately interwoven with your DNA molecules, these fears release the emotional toxins of unworthiness saturated with guilt, shame, blame, and sorrow. These two subconscious beliefs—the belief that you have been abandoned and the belief that you are unworthy to ask and to receive—produce the foundational fear paradigm. This core paradigm manifests in your reality as the lack of something that you need, especially emotional security and physical safety.

We can show you the way to break free of the lie that you are not good enough to receive from Creator. The lie originates from fear, and when fear infiltrated humankind's religions and governments, masculine ego-dominated hierarchical structures formed to control the people through fear and separation from God. The subconscious of the One Human Body contains multiple layers of beliefs that tell you that you are unworthy to receive from God. The subconscious of the One Human Body believes that Source cannot provide what is needed in daily life. We interchange the names humanity calls "God" to facilitate a reaction in your subconscious to purge the lies and fears that limit you. We will use all the following when referring to the highest vibrational energy of undiluted love: Creator, God, Mother-Father-God, Source, Divine Oneness, the Central Sun, the Central Soul, Divine Source, and the Great Universe.

Your gifted human brain responds to language in complex ways. Some words help the human subconscious to let go of fear, while other words encourage the subconscious to hold on tight. The language that we use in our communication has been carefully crafted to reveal the fear buried within you. Our words are infused with targeted healing energy that supports your conscious mind in becoming aware of the negative thought habits giving you the message that you cannot have what you desire. Consciously choosing to shift your mind's vibration out of fear and into love helps you recognize what Soul is trying to give you. As the heavy weights in your subconscious are released and forgiven, you will know without a doubt that you are worthy of asking and of receiving what is missing in your reality.

Divine human being, you need to direct the positive power of your incredible receiving force to transform your life and change the suffering that the One Human Body experiences. We assert that you have been conditioned to see yourself as lacking in value. Believing that you are not enough is displayed in your daily life as an experience of receiving your paycheck from work that does not make you happy or in having a shortage of resources to live freely. This is a problem of receiving, and this problem can be solved!

Love is the Power of the Great Universe. Love calls fear to it, and fear longs to change into love. As you live this truth and allow your humanity to receive the undiluted love energy that will materialize as what you need to be happy, your life will change in miraculous ways. We invite you to eradicate lack from your experience and witness that Soul has the power to move you into a new reality of wealth. Wealth, from our perspective, is happiness that comes with safety and security, freedom, loving relationship, self-respect, and anything else that translates as a joyful childhood, no matter your age.

We will share healing experiences in the form of visualizations that will catalyze rapid transformation and discovery. Please read these healing experiences slowly and allow the energy in the words to move your atoms. Using your creative imagination to see the scenes in the experience quickens the activation of healing. You can do this by visualizing the scenes as you read them and saying the suggested words out loud or silently to yourself. Holding the intention for the visualization to help you is just as valuable as being able to "see" what is described. We hope that you enjoy our first experience for beloved you.

Healing Experience
Receiving the Invitation

Close your eyes and take a deep breath in and exhale completely. Repeat until you feel calm and centered.

See yourself step through the purple doorway that we have opened for you. We invite you to enter our serene forest.

Walk to the circle of giant trees that have branches that touch the stars. Your divine inner child is waiting for you. Call out to the giant trees, "12 Archangels, I accept your invitation!"

The trees will turn gold and begin to sing to you. Soak up our undiluted love into every cell by repeating, "12 Archangels, I accept your invitation!"

Stay here, in Divine Oneness, until you feel hopeful and excited to receive your new life.

We invite you to RECEIVE. As you receive, you are welcoming the energy and love of Source into your reality. We thank you for helping us, through your courageous Self, to transform the suffering of the One Human Body. Let us begin by teaching you that vibration is the key to surviving in hell or thriving in Heaven, here on Earth.

Creator put laws into place that are unshakable and permanent to protect the vibration and use of undiluted love flowing to Schoolroom Earth from the Central Sun. Are you willing to witness how these highest vibrational boundaries can change your daily life? What would life feel like if you were happy, safe, purposeful, and free?

Spiritual Laws
That Help You

The divine laws are Creator's protection put into place to help guide the One Human Body through the lessons of Schoolroom Earth. All students agree to learn the qualities of undiluted love by experiencing fear in many forms, vibrations, and events. To learn what undiluted love energy is and how to use love as a healing, transforming, and manifesting power, the ego must be willing to practice unconditional loving of self and others. Learning to value that your Soul is made of undiluted love energy will restore your inner worth and lift your mind out of fear's quicksand. Fear is a negative manifesting energy, opposite in vibration to love, that magnifies itself to generate negative illusion. This negative illusion manifests in your schoolroom as suffering, drama, and separation from God. You are on Earth to use undiluted love energy to transform fear into love. As you do this, you raise your vibration and open yourself to receive from the Great Universe.

What your ego does not know until you discover it is that your ego and consciousness are the creation and expression of Soul. All Souls belong to Divine Oneness, even when fear-laden egos do all they can to separate from their Souls. Please think of the Soul as the ultimate parent for the young and rebellious ego that wants instant gratification of all it desires and control over all it experiences. Soul has vastly deep pockets of resources. Until the ego agrees to respect its parent, the ego—and the human being it represents—can experience all that fear can manifest, such as poverty, illness, shame, self-loathing, hatred of self and others, loneliness, and insecurity. When the ego gives up control and hands over the reins to Soul, the human being will experience greater ease in life on the hour.

It may appear that some egos take all they want and that if they chose to destroy Schoolroom Earth, they could do it. We want to reassure you that there is a limit to the fear these egos can use as their preferred power. Creator established boundaries that every ego, no matter how disconnected it may be from Soul, ultimately must respect. The first of the primary divine laws is As Above, So Below, As Within, So Without.

THE LAW OF AS ABOVE, SO BELOW, AS WITHIN, SO WITHOUT

Schoolroom Earth was designed to work as a perfect mirror. The vibration of Heaven (undiluted love) can also exist on Earth (love diluted with fear). Heaven's serenity and compassion are all around you. When you immerse yourself in the peacefulness and stunning beauty of Mother Nature, you are witnessing Heaven (as above) being reflected on Earth (so below). The law does not allow any fear from below to contaminate Heaven. To ensure this, the designers of Schoolroom Earth created the astral filter to capture all the manifestations and frequencies of fear. This energetic super sponge also works as a mirror reflecting into Earth's environment the mental and emotional fears of humanity. Your negative or fearful thoughts and emotions within, conscious or subconscious, show up in your "without." Your vibrations will be mirrored back to you in what you experience in your life. Depending on the frequency of what you are doing, thinking, and feeling, the astral filter will be absorbing some of the fear for you. When needed, what you have sent into the astral will be reflected in your nighttime dreams (especially nightmares).

The astral super sponge within you is the vast network of subconscious caverns where you store absorbed fear from past experiences including unhappy memories from parents, ancestors, and past lives. The subconscious, like the astral filter, is porous and can attract fear from the human collective and Schoolroom Earth, past and present. This "so within" sponge also absorbs negative and limiting thought and feeling energy generated by your ego. If you are ever in a room full of unhappy people, you can absorb their unhappiness (and likewise, if you are happy and full of love then your "so within" is reflected, "so without," into the room). Heaven's vibration of "as above" enforces the astral sponge to soak up the fear; however fear does not distinguish between the astral sponge of Earth and your subconscious. Many human beings are telepaths and empaths. They soak up the negative thoughts and heavy emotions of others (the "so without") into their own being because their subconscious (the "so within") has a memory of a similar vibration. Angels and other loving beings in Heaven clear the astral filter and the subconscious of the One Human Body frequently and fill it with undiluted love. This help from "above" lifts the vibration of the Earth and humans "below."

The great intelligence of your Soul wants to come into your ego. As you connect with Soul's intuitive Truth and listen to the guidance offered, you bring it into your ego and change what you experience in daily life (as within, so without). With each layer of fear that you transform into love, you are also bringing in undiluted love to fill the space where the fear used to hide. As you lift and transform the layers of fear and negativity that create confusion and suffering within you, you help transform the fear and negativity that causes so much destruction on Schoolroom Earth. Your choice to live in Heaven's love as much as possible positively impacts every aspect of your life and helps all others who suffer far more than your ego may comprehend.

In the Great Universe, all Souls are one. If you think of the Central Soul as an infinite lake of pure water, then every drop of water in the

lake is connected and is touching every other drop of water. When a
Soul returns to the Central Soul, it is the drop becoming part of the
whole lake again. Each Soul always retains what it has learned from
stretching far from the center of the Central Soul, and it brings its wisdom home each time it returns to Divine Oneness. This interconnectedness cannot experience true separation. No Soul is alone. Each Soul
is always included in the whole of the Central Sun and because of this,
abandonment by God is impossible. On Schoolroom Earth, this Truth
is a foundation of the cohesiveness of your education. Let us help you
understand the second primary law, the Law of One, that guides and
protects all Souls and their egos on Earth.

THE LAW OF ONE

All particles of Creator's energy exist within the body of Creator, just
like all your cells exist within the boundary of your body. All particles
of God's energy sense one another, no matter how far apart they may be
in physical space, and any energetic separation between particles is illusionary. The same is true for you. Your kidney immediately feels what
is happening in your left ear lobe. If you don't believe us, ask any cell
in any part of you, even a tiny hair follicle, and it will validate what
Angels know to be true. You are created in Creator's image and this
image is Divine Oneness. The miraculous interconnectedness between
molecules in your body works just like the interconnectedness between
stars and planets and Angels and human beings. We are all made of
particles of Creator's energy. We all live within the one Great Universe,
and it is divine law for this to be so.

When a disturbance is felt within you or anywhere on Schoolroom
Earth, Divine Oneness responds by sending undiluted love to where
it is needed. When any cell within your body shows a dip in vibration and a loss in life force, every healthy cell in your body sends
energy to the cell that has dropped in vibration. All of Mother

Nature also responds to this drop in vibration. When you stub your big toe, mountain ranges, forests, and oceans begin to send your toe healing. When there is any form of suffering in any being or dip in vibration of any particle of energy on Earth, Divine Oneness responds with help. When you willingly call on Divine Oneness to enact the Law of One, you have more power available to transform trauma or pain, including what has soaked into the spongy layers of the subconscious. As you change the suffering stored within, you help all other human beings transform their trauma, even if they are not conscious of the trauma and even if you are not conscious that you are helping them.

Many loving and healing beings have returned to Earth, intentionally taking on mental, emotional, and even physical suffering at some point during life. The Souls of these loving beings understand that their stories of pain and suffering are shared, vibrationally, with the subconscious stories found within the One Human Body. These incognito healers choose to transform the fear and forgive the hurt of their own stories knowing that they do this transformation for the greatest good of all concerned. We thank you, reader, for choosing to be one of these generously loving Souls.

The Law of One tells you that when you acknowledge that you are part of Divine Oneness, you have the power to use undiluted love to manifest, through Source, that which is for the greatest good and highest joy for all concerned. Even if the devastation and pain that your human self has experienced is vast, the Law of One tells you that you are never less than divine. As you continue to discover your innate divinity, all your suffering from all your lives will be transformed and all your scars erased. As this evolution happens, it supports the healing and evolution of all human beings, no matter how damaged or deep into fear they have sunk. As you heal and find your goodness, Mother Earth responds with miracles of planetary healing, and Divine Oneness celebrates.

All particles of energy benefit when Earth rises in vibration. Because energy cannot be destroyed, ultimately only healing, transformation, and evolution last in the big picture of your Soul's journey. You are made of energy, and it is imperative that you understand what this means.

THE LAW OF ENERGY

God/Source/Creator/Divine Oneness/the Great Universe is energy of the highest vibration of undiluted love. Love is the vibration of energy that has created all that exists in form and not in form. On Schoolroom Earth, even the darkest fear holds within it the memory of the vibration of love. Undiluted love has the power to neutralize fear and raise the vibration of fear to that of undiluted love. We tell you again that fear wants to shift in vibration and be free. Archangel Gaia, together with all the Angels of the Angelic Realms, is a vibration shifter and continuously works to repair disconnected and unaware egos. We invite you to join your highest vibrations with our energy and to assist us in transforming fear into love for the benefit of all.

Although energy cannot be destroyed, you can feel like you are losing or wasting your energy. Thoughts and emotions are made of energy and when you think thoughts of a lower vibration, even if you are unaware of what you are thinking, you can potentially lose your energy. Buried or ignored emotions will also cost you energy. Forcing yourself to earn your livelihood doing work that does not make you happy will cost you energy. The same is true for any activity that feels like an act of labor instead of an act of love.

The good news is that you can recover your energy even faster than you lose it! Thinking thoughts of gratitude and kindness, feeling emotions, and forgiving the past helps you to recover energy. Having a vocation where you enjoy being creative supports you in raising your vibration of energy to the vibration of the Central Sun. Being respectful of Mother Earth and all her inhabitants, including yourself, will raise the vibration of your energy and automatically call it to you. These simple actions in daily life will give more energy.

Time and money are not Creator's energy; however both time and money can reflect where your vibration is at any given moment. Being observant of how you spend your time and asking yourself if you are spending your time wisely shows what is happening with your energy. The same is true for money. Paying attention to how you think about money as well as noticing where there is fear present involving the receiving, earning, spending, or giving of money can be helpful to you. Human beings have been taught by others that wasting time will cost you money and vice versa. We say that earning money in a way that makes you unhappy will deplete your energy. You also may feel like it takes too much of your time. Spending your money in ways that cause you to feel that you are lacking in some way can leave you feeling depleted or anxious. Holding the vibration of undiluted love in your mind and in your humanity will help you feel that you have more time and help you trust that you will always have what you need when you need it.

Money may become an important tool for learning the value of undiluted love. Part of the earthly experience is to experiment with substituting money for God and find out if money gives you all you need to thrive as a balanced human being. Living life as if love has less value than money is very costly and quickly lowers your vibration and your self-esteem. Have you ever been seduced into believing that having financial wealth and status—or not having wealth and status—determines your self-worth and value to others? Ultimately, this subconscious and conscious evaluation causes the rapid drop in the vibration of your energy so you will feel as if you are losing energy.

Being aware of how you are controlled by time and money can help you take responsibility for what is happening to the vibration of your energy. When your vibration drops then you pull further away from the vibration of Heaven. Creating vibrational distance is the same as sinking into the lower vibrations of fear. The vibration of your energy is magnetic and Divine Oneness will feel it. You naturally draw experiences and situations that match your vibration. You need energy at the highest vibration to attract that which you desire, which also obeys the Law of One. Holding the vibration of undiluted love will help you feel like you have more time and help you receive all that you need when it comes to money, or any other resource. Does this sound familiar to you? Angels see Schoolroom Earth's most famous law, the Law of Attraction, as actually the three divine laws working in unison.

Asking to receive undiluted love from Divine Oneness into every atom of your humanity works miracles to attract Heaven's abundant flow into your everyday life on Earth. The more you ask of the Great Universe, the more God will give you what you ask for or something far better. It may not feel normal from your human perspective to ask Creator for your mundane necessities such as money, groceries, and work that you love. However, the more that you do this in tandem with transforming the fear within yourself, the more efficient your manifesting will become and the happier you will feel.

The natural expectation that your needs will be met by someone else is set up in infancy as the infant looks to the human parent figure to take care of them. When the parent cannot provide what the infant needs to feel safe, loved, and happy, the human being is starting their journey with a sense of doubt. As the infant grows, this beautiful child of God can turn the disappointment and fear of survival inward and begin to doubt their own value and believe that they are less because they are not being given the attention and affection they need. These thoughts and feelings quickly lower the vibration of a human being's energy, and they begin to attract more of the same story of disappointment, neglect, and fear. As they grow into an adult, the experience that life is not safe can become fixed, and they may see themselves as lacking or as victims that are being cheated out of a good life with no power to change their situation.

Remember, fear magnifies and makes more fear unless it is transformed with love. Love is always the healing power that you need to instantly lift your life out of fear's illusion and back into a higher vibration that will bring you what you want, not more of what you don't want.

Our mission is to teach you how to raise the vibration of your energy from the inside out and to ask Source for all you need. We will light the way for your discovery to find where the fear of the human collective is hiding within you. We will help you to lift the vibration of the old stories of suffering and unworthiness so that you think to ask God for all you need and receive even more than what you expect. The 12 Archangel way to work with the Law of Attraction is completely focused on raising your vibration. There is far more to your vibration than you may realize. We understand how the human ego wants quick results, and the fastest way to receive from Source is to have your ego fully surrender to the wisdom of the divine child that lives within you. Your divine inner child is your true essence and vibrates at the frequency of undiluted love, no matter what you may have experienced in your human childhood in this life or any other life. As your trust in your divine inner child grows, you will naturally attract into your reality Heaven's abundance in all the ways you need it to manifest tangibly. As you practice surrendering to your divinity, the One Human Body wakes up through you. You can be certain that you will experience miracles that astound you. What is a true miracle? Miracles are the divine laws of the Great Universe working through your divine inner child and team of Helpers in Heaven for your benefit and evolution.

Healing Experience
A New Beginning

Close your eyes and imagine that you are looking at yourself in the mirror. The face that is smiling back at you is yourself at around age five or six.

As you focus on the eyes of the child that is you, say, "You are the pure love of the Heart of God." Repeat this until you feel a melting and euphoric sensation fill your body. Then say, "Divine Oneness, I Am undiluted love, inside and out, and I Am calling to me that which is for my greatest good and highest joy. I Am willing to evolve into a more complete human being and through the Law of One, I desire all other human beings and all of Mother Earth to benefit from my evolution and freedom."

PART 2

Raising Your Vibration

*When fear seduces you, say, no thank you, fear. I would
rather put my energy into receiving abundance!*

THE 12 ARCHANGELS OF THE CENTRAL SUN

Definition of Wealth

We do not define wealth as your ability to acquire money in an amount that makes your ego feel secure. Wealth is your ability to receive from Source all that you need to feel safe, healthy, free, and happy. True and lasting wealth comes from the Central Sun, through your Soul to you. The inexhaustible riches of your Soul pour into your human experience as creative intelligence, and as your ego listens to your divine inner child, you learn precisely how to channel this genius into your earthly experience. As your creative intelligence is transformed into something helpful for the greatest good of all on Schoolroom Earth, then what you desire to bring into manifestation—or something even better—is given to you. The Central Sun, through your Soul, will deny your divine inner child nothing. We ask that you repeat this in your mind: "The Central Sun, through my own loving and generous Soul, will never deny me what I desire that is for my greatest good and highest joy."

Your divine inner child is the Self within that cannot be seduced by fear. This Self is the communicator for your Soul and uses the power of Heart-centered divine love and trust to raise the vibration of your mental and emotional energy when your ego and humanity fall into limitation and lack. The divine inner child needs the constant and consistent fuel of undiluted love that comes from Soul in the form of the child's parents, the divine feminine, and divine masculine. These three highest vibrational frequencies—unconditional love (divine inner child); safety, security, and creativity (divine feminine); and positive action, clarity, and focus (divine masculine)—are the Source (Soul) that takes care of you during your stay on Schoolroom Earth. You may well have experienced a surge of hope and a new awareness that lifts you out of a dark mood. This is your divine inner child, divine feminine, and divine masculine in action.

Your divine inner child is also the most trustworthy messenger for your team of Helpers in Heaven. Soul expresses innocence, intuitive feeling, and trust through the divine inner child and this Self is the symbolic spiritual Heart, the "as above" of your humanity. The mother of your divine child is the Divine Mother of the Great Universe, the feminine of Mother-Father-God/Creator/Source. The Divine Mother of the Great Universe, together with your divine inner child, lifts the vibration of your energy and receives undiluted love that then manifests as what your humanity needs and wants. Your ego cannot block this receiving when it is coming from the Divine Mother. What will you see manifest in your earthly life? The divine inner child, together with the Divine Mother of the Great Universe will receive into your life that which is for your personal greatest good and highest joy and for the greatest good and highest joy of Divine Oneness.

Does your divine inner child want to include financial freedom as an important part of your wealth? We say, yes, of course, but not so much financial prosperity that you become trapped by the money and acquisitions and forget the real Source of your joy and freedom. It can be addictive for human beings to substitute money for divine love, believing that money will give you the love and all else that you need to thrive as a contented person. The Truth is that only undiluted and consistent love can do this.

Soul reminds your ego that real wealth is having your ego depend on Soul's ability to plug into the energy of the Divine Mother of the Great Universe and receive all you need. We suggest that you begin a daily practice of inviting the Divine Mother and your divine inner child to receive lasting wealth into your reality today. How do you raise the vibration of your energy and receive abundance? Let us introduce you to the beautiful, singing colors of Mother-Father-God and the Divine Mother and the Divine Father of the Great Universe. These healing colors of undiluted love are one and the same as your chakras, batteries of the highest vibrational energy and rays of the Central Sun.

The Singing Colors of
the Central Sun

Mother-Father-God is both emotion-sound (singing) and thought-light (color). Creator uses the rays of the highest vibrational singing colors of the Central Sun to grow and care for the Great Universe. The rays of undiluted love pouring forth from the Central Sun/Soul, the Heart of Divine Oneness, come in an infinite palate, and the Angelic Realms use these rays as paint brushes that they dip into varied colors to create new scenes. We love to create new star systems and planets with lush vegetation and beautiful beings. Would you like to learn how to paint with us using the colors of the Central Sun? Come, we will show you how to create a new life where nothing is missing. We will teach you how to paint a doorway connecting you to Source so that you open to receiving more with every thought and feeling.

The receptors for receiving divine love from Source are called chakras, and these receptors exist in all of Creation. When a human being visualizes the chakra colors or holds the intention of the chakra within their Heart, the energy becomes activated and begins to expand and intensify. Although the chakras come in a vast array of colors, too many for the ego to comprehend, it may be easiest to experience the chakras as the primary colors of the rainbow: white, violets and purples, blues, greens, yellow and golds, corals and orange, and pinks and reds. You can connect with your divine inner child through visualizing the heart chakra color, emerald, and then receive from the Divine Mother of the Great Universe through visualizing the root chakra, ruby red.

By learning to work with the energy of the Central Sun through the chakras, you can facilitate deep transformation and healing for yourself as well as for the One Human Body. We will teach you how to restore your feminine (to help you to receive), rebalance your masculine (to help you focus your energy more effectively), and create a happy childhood no matter your age (connect your ego with your divine inner child and transform the hurt hiding in your subconscious).

The following sections describe where in the body the chakras are located along with the colors and qualities of undiluted love contained in each one.

EIGHTH CHAKRA

Location in the body: Sits one to two feet above your head

Colors and qualities: White and white gold bring in the qualities of purification and cleansing and help to lift up the subconscious baggage that creates lack.

SEVENTH CHAKRA

Location in the body: Sits at the crown of your head

Colors and qualities: Violet, purple, and lavender bring in the qualities of forgiveness, acceptance, and letting go and transform fear into love. Violet fire or the crown chakra energy is so powerful that it reaches ancestral fear trapped at the molecular level (DNA).

SIXTH CHAKRA

Location in the body: Sits at the third (intuitive) eye in the middle of your forehead.

Colors and qualities: Fuchsia with a dash of indigo (deepest blue) brings in the qualities of wisdom and Truth and the clarity of seeing, knowing, hearing, and sensing beyond the mundane world. Visualizing this singing color is helpful in communicating with the twin sisters of intuition and creativity. These symbolic sisters, daughters of the Divine Mother of the Great Universe, help your ego to understand the creative genius ideas coming from your Soul that will ultimately manifest freedom.

FIFTH CHAKRA

Location in the body: Sits at your throat

Colors and qualities: Sapphire blue, cobalt blue, and royal blue bring in the qualities of strength, courage, justice, respect, focus, the highest vibrational Will, and the divine masculine. Also known as the Will chakra, this chakra's energy brings in Archangel Michael (Truth and highest Will) and Archangel Victoria (divine justice and respect). These two Angels assist in clearing lies and negative and limiting attachments to the past.

FOURTH CHAKRA

Location in the body: Sits at your heart

Colors and qualities: Bright and clear greens bring in the qualities of unconditional love, spiritual growth, Trust, awakening, healing, faith in oneself and in Divine Oneness, and respect for the divinity that lives within your humanity. Activating the energy by visualizing green, together with feeling the expansive love vibration in your human heart, immediately places you in the emerald garden of Heaven with your divine inner child. This sanctuary gives you a safe place for deepest healing and for communing with your Angels and spirit Guides.

THIRD CHAKRA

Location in the body: Sits at the solar plexus

Colors and qualities: Sunny yellow, bright gold, and golden sparkles bring in happiness, personal power, self-esteem, respect, confidence, bravery, and vitality. This chakra is a supercharging energy that mixes with the other chakra energies. For example, standing in a white-gold energy waterfall is wonderful for filling up your human vessel with the pure, undiluted love of the Central Sun. Adding gold sparkles of divine love to the violet-fire energy of the crown calls in self-esteem when releasing unworthiness to receive.

SECOND CHAKRA

Location in the body: Sits just below the naval

Colors and qualities: Coral, coral pink, oranges of all shades, and scarlet bring in creative expression, creative genius and creative passion, healing from sexual abuse, and the ego-liberating energy of Soul. Coral is the receptive, feminine color of this chakra, while orange is the active, masculine Sound and Light of this energy center. Asking the Soul chakra to fire up your creative genius and Soul-driven inspiration is essential in manifesting a vocation that delights your divine inner child and provides your ego with security.

FIRST CHAKRA

Location in the body: Sits at the base of the spine

Colors and qualities: Ruby red, deep ruby pink, magenta, maroon, and scarlet Sound and Light fill every cell of your humanity with unconditional acceptance, unconditional approval, comforting love, emotional security and physical safety, and the ability to receive through the divine feminine and Divine Mother of the Great Universe. This 1st, or root, chakra grounds you to the center of Archangel Gaia. Gaia has another identity as Mother Earth. Seeing yourself soaking in a ruby lake while drinking ruby energy from a golden cup will invite in a flood of loving energy from the Divine Mother of the Great Universe. Visualizing ruby love grounds you and opens your humanity to receive from Source. Divine Mother energy is required for receiving all that makes you feel safe and secure on Earth. Her energy is needed when you desire loving relationships, good health, happiness, opportunity, and money. The ruby of the root chakra goes up your spiritual spine and fuses with the 5th, or Will, chakra. Together, these two energies create violet fire, the energy of your crown that you use for transforming your subconscious to make room within you for happiness. Abundance within you must manifest as wealth in your outer reality (daily life) because of the divine law As Above, So Below, As Within, So Without.

EIGHTH AND FIFTH CHAKRA COLOR FUSION

Sky blue brings in the qualities of clear communication, intuitive flow, and mental calmness. Mixing the fifth and eighth chakra colors creates a singing light that soothes anxiety and helps intuitive messages transform into words that you can understand with your mind and feel in your Heart. Visualizing this color invites in the Archangel of communication, Gabriel. Gabriel has another identity, the planet Mercury, and assists with listening to your divine inner child and Helpers in Heaven.

FIFTH AND FOURTH CHAKRA COLOR FUSION

Turquoise and aqua bring in the qualities of happy dreaming, freedom, and success and the manifestation of joy and satisfaction. The combination of these singing colors invites in Archangel Metatron. Metatron's other identity is the benefic planet of abundance, Jupiter. Metatron and Gabriel assist in connecting your feminine intuitive mind with God's infinite dream field of ideas. Flooding your entire being with this powerful energy of love greatly helps manifest the wealth of the Great Universe on Earth.

ALL CHAKRAS

Rainbow, opalescent, and kaleidoscope colors bring in the receiving and manifesting of a happy childhood no matter your age. Rainbow Sound and Light is an integration of all the seven primary chakras as well as those below your feet and above your head, which connect your Soul to the Central Sun. Wrapping yourself and your divine inner child in a blanket of rainbow divine love will place your ego, Heart, and Soul in perfect alignment and give your entire being a feeling of peaceful satisfaction.

We welcome you to open your creative imagination and leap into the inner realms of Heaven. We share some tools to help you work with the healing qualities of undiluted love in daily life. These tools are powerful and the more you use them, the quicker you will experience how your life changes for the better. Do not be concerned if you cannot visualize the colors and instead, use your intention to call on the energy of the chakras you need. Feeling the benefit of the divine love energy is what sets you free and the more you practice, the deeper and vaster you will experience the wonderful transforming Power of the Central Sun!

Healing Experience
Rainbow Embrace

Close your eyes and take a few deep breaths until your mind is clear.

Say, "Angels, show me what it looks like in Heaven."

A curtain lifts and you enter a magical scene of flowering trees in full bloom. The blossoms are of every color of the rainbow.

Walk among the trees and enjoy feeling the softness of the petals as they touch your hair and skin. These petals are made of divine love, and you are being showered by the Angels of the Great Universe.

Open your mouth and let a petal fall on your tongue. It tastes like your favorite flavor and as you savor the taste, your body feels so light and free.

The trees begin to sway gently in an invisible breeze and the petals from the blossoms flow into the sky above you. They mix and swirl together and sparkle with the light of the Central Sun.

The shimmering rainbow of energy in the sky creates a coat made of kindness and compassion. It falls softly from the sky and gently wraps around you. The coat of your new aura fits you perfectly. Allow the safety, security, and unconditional love of Mother-Father-God/Creator of the Great Universe/Divine Oneness to fill you with self-esteem and praise for your courage, most wondrous human being of Sound and Light!

We invite you to wear your rainbow coat of singing colors and raise the vibration of your energy. Receiving from Source will become easier as you follow our next step, which takes you even deeper into your Self. As you ask your own feminine to be restored so that she can restore your masculine and bring your brain into a new balance, you will quickly discover that your mind is not your own. Your mind, when fully connected with your Heart and Soul, becomes an open doorway connecting you to the vast resources of Heaven, the place where fear cannot exist. As you practice letting the feminine part of you lead the way forward, your outer reality will change for the better, and you will find that you have many more happy days. Let us escort you next into your feminine brain through the purple door of your crown chakra. This door is not imaginary and walking through it will change you every time you cross the threshold!

The Purple Door

The purple door is a symbolic opening located within the area of the brain called the corpus callosum. The purple door connects the masculine logical-rational brain with the feminine intuitive-creative brain when the mind is grounded by the unconditional love and Trust of the heart chakra. Why do we say the door is purple when Heart energy is emerald? When the human brain is functioning at its best vibration, the violet-fire energy of the crown chakra flows into the mind and into the nervous system cancelling fearful emotional reactions and "What if something goes wrong?" thoughts. Violet fire is the perfect balance of highest Will (sapphire blue) mixed with emotional security and physical safety (ruby red). Infusing a touch of fuchsia from the third eye chakra of intuition with violet fire creates a beautiful, rich purple.

The purple door when operating fluidly opens into the emerald meadow of Heart, and from here you have access to Heaven. Soul oversees the accessibility of the purple door. You can be certain that when control takes over your mind, the door disappears until you willingly surrender to Soul. Your divine inner child knows where the real purple door can be found, but unfortunately there can be counterfeit doors. The real purple door stays at the vibration of undiluted love while the counterfeit doors are contaminated with fear and open into the lower vibrational scenes of the astral realm or what we call ego's shadowland.

THE HIGHER VIBRATIONAL FEMININE BRAIN

Every human being has a brain that is both feminine (receptive, emotional, creative, and intuitive) and masculine (logical, rational, analytical, and task oriented). Sadly for humanity, the feminine, intuitive, creative brain—the direct pipeline to the superconsciousness of God's genius—is less popular and underused. While the door to your feminine brain is wide open in early childhood, as the ego develops, pressure from adults and older children push the door closed so that you fit the mold of what a sane and responsible human being is supposed to know and share with others. To be considered grown up and intelligent, you are taught to shut the purple door to the magical world, which is accessible only through the feminine brain. You are taught to trust only what is provable and tangible. If it can be seen with your eyes, tasted with your mouth, felt with your body, and proven by scientific fact then is it trustworthy. The masculine logical brain says be sensible, yet at lower vibrations it does not encourage using the most powerful and honest senses that you have: your intuition and creative imagination.

Walking through the purple door connects you with the infinite resources of God, and this is something the subconscious of the One Human Body believes is mostly forbidden or make-believe. Angels will tell you that choosing to believe that you live in a masculine, provable, and "concrete" world leads to poverty, misery, and unfairness. Believe in the truth of the purple door, and the door of the feminine brain will swing open on well-oiled hinges. The more you step into the emerald meadow, the easier it becomes for you to connect your ego with Heart.

Creating abundance in your daily life happens naturally and organically when you use the feminine brain and the twin sisters of intuition and creativity. Gratitude and acknowledgment for the Divine Mother of the Great Universe, your divine feminine, and divine inner child help you to receive directly from Source through the purple door into your earthly life. The purple door is an energy funnel and a miraculous vibration shifter because using the door lifts your empty baskets to where Mother-Father-God can easily fill them!

The feminine brain is where the sanctuary of the Heart is located. When allowed to function as Creator designed it, you become aware that you are God incarnated into human form. The feminine brain connects you with Angels, Mother Earth, your divine inner child, and your creative genius. When invited to lead the way, the feminine brain raises your ego and the masculine logical-rational mind out of fear and puts them in their rightful vibration of undiluted, focused love. Together, they guide your earthly life forward, out of the limiting past and into the here and now that will only get better as your ego relies on your feminine to direct your life. Using the vast treasure of the feminine brain also nurtures a youthful attitude about life and gives you faith in your own infinite power to create a happy childhood today. Let's open the purple door, raise your vibration, and receive!

❀

Healing Experience
Stepping through the Purple Door

Close your eyes and breathe in deeply and exhale completely. Focus your mind entirely on breathing in and breathing out. Repeat until you feel calm, and your mind is empty.

Say, "Thank you, divine inner child of my Heart and Divine Mother of the Great Universe, for painting a purple door for me with the singing colors of the Central Sun."

See yourself walk up to a tall purple door with a high arch at the top. Look at the door and place your nondominant hand (the hand that you do not normally use for writing) on the sparkling rainbow-crystal doorknob. Feel the coolness of the doorknob. Take a deep breath and feel the joyful energy of undiluted love flow into the palm of your hand.

Open the door and step into a brightly lit emerald field with a clear turquoise sky above. Call out to your divine inner child. Ask the child to lie down next to you on the emerald grass that feels as lush as velvet. The ground of Mother Gaia's Heart, united with the Heart of Creator, is incredibly soft and comforting. Reach out and hold the hand of your divine inner child and say, "Show me the abundant joy that you know. Teach me how to forgive the past and bring into reality the happy child-hood that you want me to experience. I thank you. I acknowledge that you are real, and I humbly ask for your help."

Feel the golden rays of the Central Sun fill every cell of your human-ity with happiness and love. Life can only get better from here on out!

EXPERIENCING THE HEALING SANCTUARY OF HEAVEN

Walking through the purple door shifts the vibration of your conscious mind and allows you to freely enter the sanctuary of Heaven located within your heart chakra. Here, you first connect with the divine inner child and together take an inventory of your energy. Every human being needs to have a flowing fountain of the Divine Mother's ruby energy of safety, security, unconditional love, and acceptance. You also need flowing fountains of positive attention, real affection, acknowledgment, happiness, and trust and faith in your Self. We suggest that you keep a fountain of divine love flowing to ensure all the other energy fountains are full. The divine love fountain fills your humanity with all you need to feel confident that yes, you do have the undeniable ability to move from lack to wealth. Checking in on your energy fountains and making sure that you are staying in the flow of divine love will greatly help you keep the vibration of your energy where it needs to be.

In the magical world of the heart chakra, your divine inner child can create these wonderful fountains where you can replenish and transform. Within the emerald meadow, you can soak in the organic palate of the heart chakra greens that sing with joy and uplift you. The heart chakra grounds you to Mother Earth at the same time. Once you feel restored, you can meet with your Angels, Guides, and Teachers in Heaven and learn all that you need to know in the here and now.

Healing Experience
Restoring in the Energy Fountains

Close your eyes, smile, and breathe. You are about to experience something truly amazing.

Say, "Thank you, divine inner child of my Heart and Divine Mother of the Great Universe, for painting a purple door for me with the singing colors of the Central Sun."

Walk through the purple door and enter the emerald meadow of your Heart.

See your divine inner child who is waiting for you next to a series of holes in the earth. These holes will become flowing fountains of healing love. Look beyond the empty holes and say, "Show me my wealth, Creator!" A huge vortex of rainbow energy will come from the sky and from the earth below and unite.

Watch your divine inner child go to the rainbow fountain and fill your cup with divine love. See the child take the cup and pour the contents into the first hole. Say with the child, "Divine Mother of the Great Universe, together with the divine feminine of my Soul, fill me with your unconditional love, safety, security, and acceptance. Watch a delicious ruby fountain rise out of the ground and reach into the sky. Take the cup from your pocket and drink from this fountain. The flavor tastes like the juice of your favorite red fruit. Drink and say, "Thank you, Divine Mother and my divine feminine, for filling every cell with your safety, security, approval, acceptance, and LOVE. I am so grateful to receive this nourishment. Thank you, Divine Mother and my divine feminine, for receiving all I need to thrive as a human being. I allow!"

Watch as the ruby fountain grows so vast and powerful that the energy starts to flow into the next hole. The energy rises from the ground in the beautiful singing colors of bright green and sunny gold.

Stand in the fountain with your divine inner child and say, "Thank you, Soul and Creator, for filling me with Trust and faith in myself and Trust and faith that I am totally supported and directed by you!"

Feel this fountain of green and gold energy grow so big that it spills over into yet another hole. Take the hand of your divine inner child and jump into the emerald pool.

Say, "I call my personal power and worth as a divine being back to me!" Gushing from the hole is a torrent of yellow and gold-sparkled singing light, and this fountain flows so high that it joins with the Central Sun. The Central Sun sends a ray of divine love into the fountain, and the vertical flow widens and rushes into every chakra of your body, even the energy centers in the palms of your hands and soles of your feet. Your divine inner child loves the happiness and joy of this powerful energy. Say, "I call my personal power, self-confidence, and worth as a divine child of the Creator into my humanity!" The yellow and gold fountain expands into the next hole. This time the energy rises from the earth in a vibrant shade of turquoise and has showers of gold light sparkles singing within it. Together with your divine inner child go and stand in this fountain and say, "Thank you, Divine Oneness, for filling me with freedom. I allow!"

And the turquoise and gold fountain of freedom bursts in size and flows into the next hole. Together with your divine inner child, watch sapphire-blue energy rise straight up as a tall shimmering blue tower of protection.

Take a deep breath and say, "I surrender to my highest Will. I desire to know my Truth and have the courage and self-respect to live it." Step into the Divine Father of the Great Universe's fountain and soak in this real acknowledgment of your authentic self. Feel the protection and invite the energy to remove all doubt from your mind.

Look into the distance and discover that the rainbow vortex of the Central Sun has now expanded to the point that it is merging with all the fountains in front of you. When they become one great fountain, stand in the undiluted love of Creator and say, "Thank you, Mother-Father-God, for filling me with happy childhood energy of the highest joy. I ask for my happiness, and I am grateful to receive. I trust that all will come to me in ways that are for my greatest good and highest joy and for the greatest good and highest joy of all concerned."

Step from God's fountain onto the lush and soft green grass. The energy of Source has transformed into the beautiful trees and fragrant flowers that have appeared in the garden of your Heart.

Invite your team of Heaven's Helpers, your Angels and Guides, to step into your sanctuary and greet you.

Angels communicate with clear intuitive thought. Be patient, breathe, and listen. They are here to help you with the next step in raising your vibration.

Keeping Watch for the Old Male and the Old Female

Because you are journeying through Schoolroom Earth, you have agreed to take on fear as your teacher. Fear's intention is to pull the ego out of alignment with Soul by putting your ego to sleep. A sleepy ego is easily convinced that he is helpless to manifest resources because Mother-Father-God does not exist on Earth. All that exists is the sleepy ego, which must do everything on his own and stay in control if he hopes to survive. We introduce you to fear's disguises that you will find inside yourself and outside in your world (as within, so without). We call these unkind and disrespectful thieves of your energy fear's old male and female archetypes. The "old" in the old male and old female refers to their ancientness in effecting human thinking and feeling responses. If you prefer, call them the dinosaur male and dinosaur female. They are fearful thoughts and lowest vibrational emotions, and they are your ego's most clever and toughest teachers. They constantly tempt you to fall into fear by seeing yourself as the victim who is not good enough, smart enough, or strong enough to live a successful and satisfying life.

HOW TO KEEP YOUR EGO AT THE VIBRATION OF DIVINE LOVE

We ask you to stay vigilant for the invasion of the old male and old female archetypes of fear and their seductive negativity that will often test you. These archetypes represent the lower-vibration thoughts, thought patterns or habits, negative feelings, and emotions that distract you from walking through the purple door. Even after you cross the threshold into your Heart, these crafty mental voices and overwhelming contracting emotions can cause disruption. You might be drawn into doubt, confusion, and shame until you have full awareness of what these heavy vibrations feel like. We encourage you to always connect with your divine inner child who lives in the sanctuary of your Heart each time you wish to enter the feminine, intuitive part of your brain. Your divine inner child will always tell you if your intuitive knowing and sensing are clear because Heart knows before your ego knows if you are ready and willing to hear the Truth.

Let us tell you more about these thieves of your wealth and how they seduce you back into lack consciousness with a mere controlling thought or wave of sadness.

FEAR'S OLD MALE

Fear's controlling-judging old male archetype lives in the rational-analytical and task-focused part of the masculine brain. He is the critical, intimidating, mental voice of pressure. He pushes you to meet deadlines, stay in control, and be judgmental of yourself and others, and he sees ruthless competition as something that motivates you to do better. He manipulates you into believing that his way of thinking and behaving protects your ego and your life from change. He loves to give orders and boss you around so that you stay on track and stay afraid of authority. He may sound convincing with his logical and seemingly well-founded complaints and observations of what is wrong. He lets you know when you don't measure up compared with another, and he encourages you to never be satisfied with what you have accomplished or with what you have acquired. His influence will tell you to never question or confront authority whether they are right or wrong and to stick with the status quo and play it safe. His criticism may remind you of your own parents or of other dominating authoritarian figures in your past.

When you hear critical thoughts in your mind focusing on all you have not achieved and pointing out all that you need to do but are not doing, recognize this as the voice of the old male. This demanding emperor speaks the negative, fear-inducing language of "not enough." His language is spoken repeatedly by his army of judging thoughts that demand all vulnerable egos to quake in their boots and bow down to his authority. The boss of the ego will always tell you to do more of what you are not doing enough of to be successful in the world of men.

The controlling-judging old male has no place for creativity, intuition, imagination, or hopefulness. To him, this is nonsense and impractical. The father of the ego can make your choices for you if you do not silence him. He can instantly have you believing that asking for help in receiving what you need from the Great Universe, especially from Angels and Helpers in Heaven, is weak and a waste of precious time. He tells you to simply do a better job of controlling your life. Have you witnessed the global old male archetype playing his tricks on the world stage? We see him seeking power and control as the hierarchical patriarchy that rules many religions, corporations, and world governments. Any of the singing colors of the Central Sun turn him to dust, and he especially does not care for the energy of the crown chakra (violet fire), the energy of the third-eye chakra (fuchsia singing light), or the energy of the root chakra, (ruby flame).

FEAR'S OLD FEMALE

When the ego is lacking in perfection, the controlling-judging old male calls in the crippling old female archetype to fill your mind and body with guilt, shame, helplessness, and anxiety. The old female encourages you to be the silent, self-neglectful servant who hides their resentment and jealousy of those who have what you want but do not have. This negative inner mother will have you consumed by self-loathing and unworthiness unless you forbid her from taking over your vulnerable ego. She is the humiliating inner voice of shame and rejection as she whispers in your ear to blame yourself or blame another for why you are lacking or feeling mistreated. As you find yourself sinking into despair, she tells you that you deserve to be miserable and poor. This self-appointed and highly entitled mean queen is the generator of both lack and victim consciousness for your ego. The old female, together with the old male, will make you think and feel that you have less intelligence, ability, and opportunity than others and that your best hope is to find someone who will take care of you if you sacrifice your life to be the caregiver. When either the old male or old female archetypes are active in your brain, your ego may find himself needing approval of your value from others, feeling needy for acknowledgment, and using all that is wrong as a way to receive attention. Do you want the old male and the old female to be the inner parents for your ego? Tell them, "Thank you, but I already have parents helping me with my life. My divine feminine and divine masculine are all I need!"

And do these characters leave the ego alone when life improves? To be honest, they will get stronger. Please remember that the old male and old female are archetypes of fear. As you continue to discover your inner worth and stand up to the old male and old female, they will try to make you feel anxious about the future and frustrated that you are not as free and happy as you want to be right now. They will try to make you feel uncomfortable when you are having fun, being creative, and making progress with living a more balanced life. They teach you a very important lesson: to stay mindful of the vibration of your thoughts and feelings and not accept their presence in your humanity. They will be your teachers until you no longer need them because you have learned to move out of not-good-enough consciousness and value the vast worth of your own self every day.

The dissatisfaction and negativity that come from the controlling-judging old male and guilt-mongering old female can be felt by others. Likewise, you feel the fear generated by these characters from the entire human collective. Although the hurts from the old male and old female are in the past, these wounds and fears propel into the future. They leave you feeling deeply insecure that you will not have what you need tomorrow, next month, or ever. You have the ability and the strength to change this story of all-pervasive insecurity and doubt, and we intend to prove this to you. The 12 Archangels of the Central Sun embrace you and your hurts with unconditional love and compassion. We will teach you how to change the vibration of toxic energy so that you resonate with the vibration of Heaven. We only need the willingness of your ego and your courage to say no to the demands of the old male and old female. We request that you read the following healing experience as needed. Think of it as a kind and loving gift that your divinity is giving to your humanity.

Healing Experience
Love Alarm

Close your eyes and breathe.

Walk to the purple door and open it. Do not step through the door. Ask your divine inner child and guardian Angels standing in the emerald meadow to cross over into your masculine mind.

One of your Angels picks up your divine inner child and together they pull the ruby red fire alarm that is located to the left of the purple door.

The rainbow lights come on. Listen to the joyful music playing from invisible speakers. Grumpy old men (fear-based thoughts) and bitter old women (lower-vibration emotions) scramble to avoid the glorious white-gold divine love pouring out through the purple door.

Say, "Thank you for teaching me to stay mindful of my thoughts and feelings! Now OUT! OUT! OUT! I call on the power of the divine laws, and with this power, I command you to leave my head, my body, and my humanity, NOW!"

The tidal wave of violet fire, energy that transforms fear into love, floods your body. The old male thoughts and old female feelings and emotions lift out through the top of your head and are carried straight to the magnificent Central Sun shining above you.

Cross the threshold of the purple door with your divine inner child and guardian Angels into the emerald sanctuary of Heart. Ask your divine inner child, "What do I need to receive from the Great Universe today?"

The Healing Gifts
of the Divine
Inner Child

We encourage you to begin each day saying, "I invite my divine inner child to show me how to fully surrender my ego to the joy of Soul. Thank you, divine inner child, for helping me to remember that I am a child of the Divine Mother of the Great Universe. Thank you, Heart and Soul, for filling my entire being with the healing energy of love and comfort that you offer me. I am grateful that the Divine Mother is my true mother and that you want me to feel safe, secure, and loved." Holding the intention to stay connected with your divine inner child will help your ego recognize messages of Truth coming through your intuitive knowing. As the messenger of your Soul and connector to the pipeline of abundance coming through the divine feminine, your divine inner child is the key that unlocks the treasure you have been waiting to receive. Ask your divine child, the higher Self that your ego can relate with, to receive from Source. You will swiftly discover that God has not abandoned you.

WHO IS THE DIVINE INNER CHILD TO ME?

The divine inner child has the voice and appearance of yourself as a child and can appear to you at any age that is needed to convey the message the ego needs to hear. Sometimes this child may appear (or feel) to be very young if she is trying to let you know that you need to ask Mother-Father-God to fill your humanity with safety. At a different time, she may appear to be a teen or young adult because she wants to communicate a genius idea that will allow you to create something wonderful that will be for the greatest good and highest joy for Divine Oneness. The divine inner child is both a doorway to access the superconscious and an opening to your subconscious. When the door opens to your subconscious, your consciousness can be flooded with memories of hurt and unfairness from this life. If you keep the door open, you can access memory of events in past lives and events from the lives of your ancestors. Because your divine inner child is fearless, she can become the all-knowing ancient one that is the head librarian of your vast subconscious libraries. She grants you the ability to hear the laments of the wounded self through her, so that you know what stories are ready to be transformed, released to the Central Sun, and forgiven even if they seem unforgiveable.

HEALING THE SEPARATION BETWEEN THE EGO AND SOUL

Acknowledging your divine inner child releases the Heart Power to move your ego to surrender and heal. This journey of surrendering to Soul and healing the separation between the ego and Soul is required to live as a happy and safe child, no matter your age and no matter the pain and loss you have suffered. Connecting Soul to the ego begins with asking your divine inner child, "What am I feeling? What is it that I truly need?" You may hear an answer from your divine Self that tells you all is harmonious. You may hear an answer from your wounded self that tells you what is now ready to be forgiven and given to the Central Sun for transformation.

We ask that you see transformation—using undiluted love to change fear into love—as the pure water that allows the seed to grow and blossom into the lovely flower of your true authentic self. We are hopeful that you will quickly discover that you are a divine human being and you lack nothing. Everything that you need and want to be happy needs to be validated by your divine inner child because this highest and most innocent Self knows and feels what matters most to you. Your Soul needs your ego to evolve and evolving requires that you choose love over fear. Your divine inner child knows how to guide you so that you see the choice and feel the choice before you put yourself in a compromising and painful story that often is an emotional repeat of the past. Let your divine inner child Self become your best friend and most trusted spiritual guide and experience far more of Heaven's abundance in your daily life.

Healing Experience
Receiving Guidance and Healing

Close your eyes and focus on your breathing until you feel calm and centered.

Walk through the purple door and enter the emerald sanctuary of your Heart.

Archangel Michael of the Central Sun greets you and lovingly sends his sapphire blue Sword of Truth and Awareness down your spine and grounds the sword in the earth beneath your feet. Sparkles of gold, undiluted Central Sun love flood your mind and body.

Archangel Michael then escorts you to a human-sized lotus blossom that has fully bloomed. Look for your serene divine inner child who is sitting in the blossom, smiling and wise.

Your divine feminine and masculine appear sitting on either side of your divine inner child. Archangel Michael tells you to sit across from them, and he sits next to you. His huge sapphire wings of singing light gently embrace you, and you feel like your personal space has expanded to a refreshing vastness.

Ask your Soul these questions and let the answers flow softly into your consciousness through your intuitive knowing. Trust what you hear and know the answers will repeat if needed.

What am I feeling emotionally? What do I need to feel but resist feeling? (If the feeling has a lower vibration, forgive it and release it to the Central Sun).

What do I need to feel safe, secure, free, happy, and abundant? Is there anything that my ego thinks that I need but is a distraction or not good for me?

Am I being tricked or pulled into a lower vibration by the old male or old female? If so, please explain how.

Is there a story from my past that I am ready to release, forgive, and transform so that I can receive wealth from you?

And last, are all my fountains of divine love flowing? Divine Mother's safety and security? Green and gold fountain of Trust and faith in myself? Yellow and gold fountain of inner worth and personal power? Turquoise and gold fountain of freedom? Sapphire-blue fountain of protection and Truth? And the rainbow geyser of undiluted love to keep me completely saturated with loving-kindness for myself and others?

Once your questions have been answered, rest in the lotus and allow your humanity to soak up the love offered into every thought, feeling, belief, and dream of your Heart.

You are now ready to understand where your lack consciousness comes from so that you can transform it, layer by layer, lie by lie. Please think of your vessel—body, mind, Heart, and Soul—as a treasure chest that is vast in size and depth. Some of this treasure is lead that must be turned into gold. Your ancestors thank you for doing this alchemy for them. Humanity thanks you, and all of Heaven helps you. Let's make more room inside of you to receive your abundance from the Great Universe!

Changing the Repetitive Story of Lack

Before you incarnated, you designed your karmic homework and planned out events that would happen in life to test your faith in undiluted love. Prior to arrival on Earth, you knew that life experiences would require learning to practice forgiveness, unconditional love, and patience. Ultimately, successfully completing your homework, or karma, requires relying on Source to furnish everything you need. Depending on how Soul created your lessons, you may have experienced a shortage of material and emotional resources as early as conception. You, most wondrous divine human being, began as a cell from your mother and a cell from your father. Contained within the zygote of you were the subconscious fears and insecurities of each of your parents. If either parent experienced poverty or suffering inherited from their own ancestral linage then these fear-laden memories were downloaded into your cells. When your mother had any anxiety during her pregnancy, you experienced her fear. Her tension of not feeling secure and safe began to enter your awareness and became a part of your developing nervous system. Feeling afraid is a natural and organic feeling to you. Not constantly feeling safe in utero and during development can generate doubt about your ability to thrive in life. Let us explain.

When material and emotional resources are missing or in short supply during development and childhood, you lose confidence and trust in Soul's intelligence to take care of you. The shortage of emotional support, love, attention, and acknowledgment has the greatest impact on your security as a growing human being. You may not have had robust health and vitality as a child, or you may have felt shy and clumsy. Not feeling empowered, capable, and protected in your early environment can turn into the expectation that life is hard. Insecurity about whether you will flourish can generate constant anxiety about the future. When you do not feel safe as a fetus, infant, young child, or young adult, then your work to transform the fear of not having enough multiplies exponentially. Where there is a fear of survival, trust in Source is missing. Trust must be restored before your Heart will open to receiving the love of the Divine Mother. When your primary (molecular) response is not to trust, we thank you for your relentless determination to reconnect with Soul. Doing this, restoring your broken humanness with the powerful healing energy of Trust, transforms your own life and greatly helps the One Human Body. You can be sure that Divine Oneness is helping you to restore your trust in Source. Trust, in Soul and in Source, is the alchemical power that works to change the old story of not having what you need to truly thrive. Say within your Heart, "My story of lack is not my fault. My inability to trust that Creator will provide all I need is not my fault. I am innocent and I am willing to transform the fear that limits me, for the greatest good of all."

Unworthiness, shame, guilt, and the fear of punishment, each a warrior of fear, soak into the bones of your humanness. These fierce monsters gobble up the goodness of what you desire to receive from Source. Fear's warriors are nearly always rooted in religious doctrines archaic in origin and insidious in action. These deep subconscious messages are fear's toxic waste that require alchemical transformation using undiluted love. We are going to teach you how to do an unparalleled shift in your vibration. Yes, you can eliminate these ancient negative voices that can hold you prisoner in lack consciousness from deep within.

Healing Experience
Transforming Subconscious Unworthiness and Guilt

Close your eyes and breathe in deeply and say, "Rise up guilt, shame, fear of punishment, and unworthiness!" And then exhale slowly and completely. Please repeat a few more times.

Walk through the purple door and find your divine inner child waiting for you in the emerald meadow of your healing Heart.

Together, walk up the small hill and look down at the gently flowing violet-fire river below. Lie down and place your divine inner child on your human heart and roll down the hill and right into the river. It is made of the energy of forgiveness, and it feels like landing in pillowy love.

Stand up in the river of forgiveness and transformation. Take the small hand of your divine inner child and notice that we, the 12 Archangels, are encircling both of you. Invite the violet-fire river to rise to your chin.

Say, "I release the unworthiness, guilt, shame, victimization, and fear of punishment wherever it is stored within me. I release it. I forgive it, and I send it to the Central Sun."

Continue to release and forgive until the river changes in color from violet to turquoise. See the sunlight expand above your head and know that it will not hurt your eyes to look directly into it.

Together with your divine inner child reach up into the light of the Central Sun and pull the undiluted love into your body. See and feel yourself being lit from the inside out. Say, "Thank you, Central Sun of Divine Oneness, for restoring my self-worth and for filling me with respect and gratitude for me."

Invite the turquoise energy of expanding self-worth, freedom, and manifestation to flow into the cells of your being. Allow the turquoise river to rise far above your head and know that as we surround you in a circle you can breathe freely.

Say, "Thank you, Central Sun of Divine Oneness, for filling me with freedom, happy childhood, good vibrations, and self-confidence."

Once we see that you are glistening turquoise and full of golden happiness, we will lift you out of the river and place you and your divine inner child gently on the top of the hill. Look down at the river . . . it has now become a rainbow of delight for you. Call the rainbow energy of undiluted love to you and watch it replenish every cell of your precious humanity.

Now that the frequency of your energy is at a loving vibration, we have someone that you need to befriend—your wounded self. This self is so very worthy of receiving your unconditional love and help. The wounded child self opens the passageway into the forgotten and hidden caverns of your subconscious. Loving the unlovable and for-giving the unforgivable will be asked of you. We hope that you find it invaluable to transform the hurts of the wounded self. We ask that you think of this as letting go of unwanted things in your closet and making room for new items that express who you are now. If you could see the vastness of your potential through our eyes, you would know that more Heaven knocks at the door to come in, and we thank you for making room!

THE WOUNDED SELF, OPENING THE STORAGE VAULT OF LACK

The wounded self is the cautious and protective guardian of your sub-conscious libraries and the defense system for your self-limiting pat-terns of behavior. Powerful, secretive, and hurting, this self decides which memories and outdated belief paradigms have permission to pass through the subconscious veil and enter your conscious awareness. Once the light of consciousness and undeniable truth has shined the light on the past, you have the choice to forgive it and let it go or repress it and pretend that the past has no influence on your negative habits. Why would you choose to hold on to the wounds of the past? Holding on to memories of hurt and fear can serve the wounded human as an illusionary form of protection from future trauma. Not the most joyful and free way to live, fear sells the wounded self a way to survive a potentially dangerous situation. Every human being needs to feel safe and secure and to receive positive attention and trustworthy affection, unconditional love, and acknowledgment of their worth to the family. When you do not receive these key ingredients needed for healthy growth, you learn how to manipulate yourself and sometimes others in order to survive. For example, if learning how to anticipate the needs of others provided you with some positive attention and acknowledgment or offered some protection from humiliation, then you may still feel the need to please others. Not receiving the support needed as a child may have you living a life where there is insufficient safety, emotional security, unconditional love, and happiness. Understand that the unhealed wounded self stays in survival mode, even when the emotional environment is harmonious.

Nonjudgment, kindness, and patience will eventually convince the wounded self to open the vault to the fear-based beliefs that block or limit receiving from the Great Universe. Trust energy, a quality of undiluted love creates a bridge between the deep subconscious and the conscious mind. Trust must be established between the wounded self, especially when this self is a child, and the Heart. Once the wounded self feels safe enough to crack open the door, only then will the deepest buried memories of lack and suffering be revealed and permitted to be released for healing by love from Soul. How do you convince this heroic gatekeeper to trust that healing, not suffering, is at hand? We encourage you to communicate to your wounded self and acknowledge this self's innocence and divinity, no matter what their reason is for the regret, fear, or guilt. Saying often, "I forgive it all, even if I don't know what needs to be forgiven" is profoundly helpful in transforming the hurt trapped in the subconscious. Practicing forgiveness along with calling on the help of Angels and trusted loved ones in Heaven will help your subconscious purge the heavy suffering and sorrow that has been creating any repetitive story of disappointment.

Healing Experience
Healing the Wounded Self

Cross your arms over your chest and hold yourself in a gentle hug. Close your eyes and say, "I love you, my brave hero that has helped me to survive for so very long."

Ask your guardian Angels and the 12 Archangels to bathe your humanity in loving-kindness and feel a soft pink energy flood your body. Say, "Disappointed and all alone self within me, I acknowledge you and I need your help and guidance more than ever."

Focus again on feeling the loving-kindness fill you.

Say, "Thank you for releasing the old stories, traumas, and patterns that we have outgrown. Thank you for being my guide and the Angel within me who sets me free to experience happiness and freedom."

Ask Mother-Father-God to fill your humanity with the trust that the healing is happening and that you are ready to receive far more from the Great Universe. Say, "I Am so grateful for this healing. I Am so grateful that I am receiving more from the Great Universe every day."

TRANSFORMING SURVIVAL-BASED BELIEFS LODGED IN THE DEEP SUBCONSCIOUS

Fear's old male and old female, together with your wounded self, use the fear and loss of the deep subconscious as fuel to torment you with the belief that you are not enough and there is not enough of what you need. When the wounded self, in survival mode, is trying to protect you from a change perceived as dangerous, the old male will fill you with controlling, judging, and critical thoughts. The old female will usher in guilt, unworthiness, and shame. All this fear has the power to limit what you allow yourself to receive from Source. It also can keep you in a state of loss and pain because the suffering is familiar. The old male, old female, and wounded self will try to convince you that the suffering, even if it makes you miserable, is the safest way to live your life. Meanwhile, your ego can grow increasingly frustrated that all your prayers seem to be going unanswered. Yes, human being, fear wants you to believe that God is deaf when it comes to hearing you.

We ask that you think of your deepest, survival-based fears as the "devils" that you and your Soul want to vanquish so that you can experience true safety and security. Often these fears have been inherited through ancestry, brought in from past lives or from hurtful experiences in childhood. Here is our list of what makes you believe that you are not enough and resist asking Creator for what you want and need. Sometimes your desire is squelched before it even reaches your conscious mind.

LACK BEGINS AS THE SUBCONSCIOUS BELIEF, "I AM NOT ENOUGH"

We ask that you think of your human vessel as having accumulated mud at the bottom of it. The mud of not enough is taking up space that wants to be filled with the trust that God will take care of you as a beloved and valued child. Transforming the ancient and hard layers of mud that represent unpleasant experiences of the past is an essential process to end the repetitive story of lack.

If in the past asking God or another human being for what you wanted caused emotional or physical trauma, your subconscious may believe that asking for what you need is forbidden and hopeless. Let's use an example that you were a healer in a past life who trusted your direct access to Creator's healing power, yet your ability was seen as a threat to the patriarchal church. The authorities shamed you and your family in public for sins against God. To teach a lesson to others, you were found guilty and imprisoned, which left your family destitute and in exile from society. Can you see why your subconscious would try to prevent you from having a conscious connection with Source in this life, one where you feel safe in asking and receiving for all you need? Your subconscious has its reasons for holding on to the memories and the fears of the past; however, these beliefs are often detrimental to your present life. To recover your true worth and transform the lack consciousness you carry in your cells, we ask you to peruse a list of what could be stored in the depths of your subconscious. If you feel a reaction in mind or body, then you have some releasing and forgiving to do. Forgiving allows the peeling away of the layers of hurt and fear. The wounded self is on a journey to transform into your Self.

Below is our list of subconscious beliefs along with a few real or perceived experiences that can keep the story of lack repeating. If you were neglected, abandoned, or abused in childhood, these fear-based beliefs can create a fortress of resistance to change. The cleansing energy of your chakras can dissolve the fortress around your Heart; however, it takes patience and love to achieve.

As you read through the list of hidden beliefs, your feminine intuitive brain will recognize the beliefs that are stored in your deep subconscious. Every time that you read the list, you may feel a response to a belief that you did not feel before. By reading the list slowly and carefully, you are supporting your feminine brain to wake up your memory. Your body will give you a signal of recognition. This may be a kick in the gut, a contraction in your heart area, or just a knowing within that says, "I feel that this is inside of me." With each recognition comes a hidden fear that says, "In order to survive, I must hold on to this belief." Our good news is the violet fire of the Central Sun takes care of all of it!

► Root Causes of "I Am Not Enough"

The following are examples of subconscious beliefs:

- You do not have what it takes to survive in life
- You are not safe to feel your emotions and to acknowledge what you feel
- You are a disappointment
- You have no value and that you are unwanted
- You are less than because your parents or family have addictions, abuse, or other painful stories in their pasts
- You deserve to be punished or you will be punished even if innocent
- You are not good enough
- Because you are a human being, you are less than God
- Poverty or another form of suffering is necessary for purifying the ego-human self
- You were unwanted by your parents (may be an actual experience)
- Everyone in your family struggles with financial hardship (may be an actual observation)
- Those in financial debt avoid laziness because debt is a good motivator
- Getting out of financial debt is difficult to accomplish
- Because you are a female, you are dependent on a male
- If you are not dependent on someone, you will be alone in life
- You are unworthy of receiving from Source
- You failed yourself or another in this life
- You committed an unforgivable crime or sin
- You have not done enough for others
- You are unlovable and undeserving
- You are lacking in intelligence

- You are lacking in ability
- You are lacking in attractiveness
- You are lacking in youth
- You are lacking in wisdom and intuitive ability
- You are lacking in creativity
- You are lacking in time, energy, and focus
- You cannot get enough accomplished and, therefore, something must be wrong with you
- Your position in life is to be the servant or slave
- You are here to be the hero, no matter the cost
- You must take care of others before caring for yourself
- You must be the responsible one and sacrifice what you want to do when what you want to do conflicts with being the responsible one
- Depriving yourself of what you need and want is a smart way to conserve your money
- Depriving yourself of what you need is helpful to someone else or helpful for protecting you from harm from others
- You have been neglected and that neglect, even by the Great Universe, is the story of your life
- You must be the peacekeeper
- You are being disrespectful if you ask for what you need or want from another person, especially a parent, or from Mother-Father-God
- You are guilty
- You should feel ashamed
- What you are here to share is not wanted by others and therefore it is very difficult to earn a living by doing what you love to do
- You are bound to stay in the work that provides a steady paycheck but makes you miserable
- You must give more than what you receive to be loved by God
- You must give more than what you receive to be loved by another person

- You are helpless
- The Great Universe does not have what you need
- You are not allowed to have what you want
- Someone will take what you have away from you
- The government or religious authority will punish you if you do not live in lack
- The government or religious authority will punish a member of your family if you attract attention due to wealth
- Being afraid keeps you "on the straight and narrow"
- Wealth will draw unwanted attention to you from family, friends, or peers
- You belong to a particular socioeconomic group (family, tribe, community) and are not allowed to do better than those of this group
- If you have all you need to be happy, you will become self-absorbed and lazy
- All financially wealthy people become selfish
- You are self-centered if you desire to be acknowledged and valued for what you give
- Creator does not step in and help with matters of earthly life

Here are some examples of real or perceived experiences:
- Being abused or fearing that you will be killed for asking for what you want or need; or having the memory of being killed for doing so in another life
- Being a victim and failing to rise above it
- An intimate relationship ending in betrayal and heartache
- Physical punishment
- Angels not showing up for you

Any of these beliefs and experiences can be entangled with others on the list, and the compounded fears can create a story of lack that is confounding and frustrating to change. We ask that you read through the following two healing experiences slowly and deliberately and do them until you feel comfortable asking Source for what you desire to be a happy child, no matter your age. We also ask that you continue the healing experiences until you transform the not-good-enough thoughts that tell you there is not enough for you to flourish in daily life.

Doing the first exercise helps the most elusive beliefs to begin to come out of hiding. The second exercise targets lack beliefs that you have inherited. As you repeat these exercises, new limiting beliefs will come up from the subconscious to be transformed. Feel your feelings, release, and forgive. Note that the healing works even if you find visualization challenging.

Healing Experience
Transmuting Lack Beliefs

You may want to read through the exercise a few times. Feel free to pause as needed.

Close your eyes, take some deep, centering breaths and step through the purple door. Look for your divine inner child, divine feminine, and divine masculine and follow them to the big spiral staircase that leads to the vast subconscious library.

Climb the stairs, enter the library, and stop at the front desk. Your guardian Angel librarian is waiting to escort you into the great hall of the library.

With the help of your divine inner child, check the potted plants for any hiding old males and old females. Your divine inner child carries a spray bottle filled with ruby and gold energy of the Divine Mother. The old male and old female will dissolve instantly with every spray.

Walk into the great hall and again, look for the old male and old female archetypes of fear. You know what to do with them. Look up at the towering shelves of storybooks. Many of the books contain subconscious memories with negative subconscious beliefs. Some of the books contain pages of the story you are living in this life with current beliefs and expectations recorded in the chapters. There are also many rooms that connect with the great hall.

Look around the great hall and see and feel us—the 12 Archangels of the Central Sun have come to help you. We have placed a huge violet-fire dumpster, lined with sapphire-blue coals in the bottom, in the middle of the great hall. Leading from the violet-fire dumpster is a conveyor belt that will take the most crystalized stories to the Central Soul of God.

Ask us to help you find the stories of lack on the shelves. Toss the books into the violet-fire dumpster and say, "I release this old story. I let it go entirely and I forgive it, even if it feels unforgivable to forgive."

Ask your divine masculine to look around for the old male and old female and if any are found, we will put them in the dumpster and transmute them for you. Make sure to throw their backpacks into the violet-fire dumpster, as they are full of comparing thoughts, judging thoughts, not-enough thoughts, powerless and helpless thoughts and feelings, and feelings of despair, resentment, envy, loss, and shame.

Once all the sad stories have been transformed, ask your wounded selves and the wounded children of your ancestors to come out from the rooms joined to the great hall.

The violet-fire dumpster has now been transformed into a violet-fire waterfall with ribbons of the colors of the rainbow flowing down into a ruby pool. Invite your wounded selves and the wounded children of your ancestors to step into the ruby pool, underneath the colorful waterfall of divine love, with you and your divine inner child, divine feminine, and divine masculine.

Say, "I release and I forgive all the grief and loss, resentments and traumas from my past and from the past of my ancestors. Together, we let the lack go and we say, "I Am more than enough to ask and receive from Source. I Am more than enough to receive from Divine Oneness all I need and want to be happy, free, and abundant!"

Listen to us sing and watch us expand the energy of the waterfall and the ruby pool until all becomes the pure energy of undiluted love. Bask in the healing waters. Once the healing is complete, you will find yourself resting in the emerald meadow of Heart.

Healing Experience
Releasing Ancestral and Past-Life Trauma

This exercise can be done at bedtime. Once you are comfortably in bed, close your eyes and see yourself walk through the purple door. Submerge yourself in a magnificent violet-fire ocean of healing energy. The ocean is saturated with ruby and gold sparkles and in the not-too-far distance is a circle of 12 Great Angels wearing the singing colors of the Central Sun.

Together with your divine inner child, swim toward our circle of undiluted love, and lie down on the ruby bed we have prepared for you. As you rest in the bed, please say, "I release it all. I forgive it all. I forgive it for all of us." We will scrub the old stories of fear, trauma, punishment, pain, suffering, loss, grief, and the lie that you are separate from Source out of your DNA molecules.

Repeat, "I am willing to experience a happier childhood, at my present age, by the time I wake up in the morning."

Sweet dreams most loved and cherished child of Divine Oneness. Sweet dreams!

PART 3

Receiving Your Wealth

All Divine Oneness lives in abundance. You are part of Divine Oneness.

THE 12 ARCHANGELS OF THE CENTRAL SUN

What Does Wealth Look Like to You?

The essential question to ask is, "What is missing from my reality that will make my life on Schoolroom Earth feel like I am living in peaceful serenity?" Asking the question invites your ego to engage with your Soul, without triggering defensiveness and resistance. Your divine inner child, divine feminine, and divine masculine know what is missing for your ego and for your humanity. Moving past the resistance of the ego helps you to receive your abundance from the Great Universe. The tricky part may be that your ego believes it already knows what will bring happiness, freedom, a sense of security, and inner peace. The ego may think that it knows exactly how to make this happen. When the ego wants to go in a direction that gives it power and control, and Soul is guiding your life to take a far easier path, there can be a vibrational conflict of interest. When this happens, your outer reality, from your ego's point of view, will look like nothing is changing and that life is disappointing and difficult.

How can you merge what your ego longs to experience with the bigger needs of your humanness as perceived by your Soul? By understanding the roots of what is motivating your ego to want what you want. For example, did you know that when your ego is in despair about money, the root of the issue is that you need the love of the Divine Mother of the Great Universe? Asking, first, to be filled with her love and, second, voicing that you need a financial miracle will bring exactly what you need and in a way where you do not feel punished. If your subconscious holds the belief that you are not allowed to ask for money, especially from God, then your ego, without knowing it, may bring in the money through a high-interest loan or through work that causes you to suffer. We have one more example for you: if your ego desires something expensive that says to others, "I am important and you need to pay attention to me," the core need is for acknowledgment from the Divine Father of the Great Universe. Asking to be filled with unconditional love, respect, and acknowledgment from the Divine Father will attract to you the recognition and opportunity that you seek. If you ask for a fill up from the Divine Mother and from the Divine Father of the Great Universe, then you will experience receiving in the funds needed to dress you for success. However, this time, the new suit of clothes will matter to you because it will be something that you choose with your Heart and makes you smile when you wear it. Let's look at some core motivations that make a significant impact on what your ego desires. The divine Law of As Above, So Below, As Within, So Without will always work in your favor if you ask for your true needs to be met.

SUBCONSCIOUS MOTIVATIONS INFLUENCING WHAT YOU BELIEVE YOU WANT

The most foundational subconscious motivation is the need for safety and security regardless of whether there is an actual lack of safety and security. This subconscious belief paradigm is rooted in the expectation that Creator might abandon you or that your tribe, community, or family might abandon you if you are seen as unacceptable. To recognize if this subconscious need is influencing what you think you want, check in to see if you are feeling fearful about the future. Do you have anxiety that you cannot explain or a need to be in control as much as possible? Is it challenging for you to trust yourself and to trust others, even if you know they are trustworthy? Do you struggle with knowing what you want for yourself? Often there is the motivation to be self-sacrificing, self-denying, and self-rejecting hidden underground.

When there is a deep fear of not having enough combined with a fear of being abandoned, your ego may feel unsettled with making decisions around money or food. When there is an unmet need for safety and security, and doubt concerning your lovability, then it may be uncomfortable to save, spend, share, and receive money.

Healing Experience
Releasing the Expectation of Being Abandoned by Creator

Close your eyes and breathe in deeply and exhale slowly. Focus on your breath until it finds a peaceful rhythm.

Walk through the purple door into the emerald sanctuary of your Heart. Find your divine inner child, divine feminine, and divine masculine and together step under the violet-fire waterfall of transformation and forgiveness. Refocus on your breathing.

Say, "I welcome all of my subconscious and conscious concerns that I have been abandoned and do not have enough of what I need to feel safe, emotionally and physically, to be released from my being. I send all of my fears and negative expectations to the Central Sun."

Stay in the violet-fire waterfall repeating, "I forgive it all" until the waterfall changes color to a vibrant ruby. Open your mouth and drink in the Divine Mother's unconditional love, safety, true security, and comfort. Allow your entire body to be saturated with Divine Mother's healing love.

When you are ready, ask your divine inner child to tell you what you need, here and now, on Schoolroom Earth. Give thanks that you are receiving it even if it has not manifested.

◇◇◇

Another important subconsciously driven motivation can be caused by the core needs for positive attention, real acknowledgment, and trustworthy affection not being met. When these primary needs have been neglected, you may find yourself struggling with any of the following: physical illness, suffering, loneliness, poverty, repeated job loss, overworking, financial struggle, and addiction. Your ego may not be able to buy enough gifts to satisfy the deep yearning to be wanted and valued. When either the first or second subconscious motivation stories are activated, the ego may never be satisfied with all that you have now, or with the wealth you receive in the future. Being filled with what you need will support your life in a consistent, sustainable way so that you never want for anything again.

Healing Experience
Filling Up with All You Could Ever Want

Close your eyes and breathe naturally. Smile and wrap your arms around yourself and repeat, "I love you. I love you. I really love you."

Walk through the purple door and look for the beautiful tree with blossoms of many colors. Find your divine inner child who is beckoning to you.

First hug the tree. Hug the tree and feel it's great, vast, and infinite love and affection for you. Climb the tree and sit next to your divine inner child. Hug each other and acknowledge your intelligence, good looks, courage, talent, and all things that need to be acknowledged. Listen for more acknowledgment to come from your divine feminine-mother and divine masculine-father.

Ask your guardian Angels to carry you higher into the tree. We will meet you at the very top and show you endless wonderful things about you, through your own higher awareness. We will fill you with Creator's affection and so much sunny attention that you might blush. Enjoy it. It is well deserved!

Freedom to be your true authentic self and to live your life as you choose inspires what you want your wealth to look like and how you want abundance to manifest. Where there has been a history of ancestral, past-life, or current-life trauma, the need for freedom can be the strongest of all motivators. When the requirement for freedom influences the ego from deep within, you may find long-term commitments challenging. It may be frustrating to do work that you do not love. You may prefer to live and work independently because you need to do things your way. Wealth needs to come to you in a way that liberates your life from stress, not in a way that adds more responsibility to your already "full plate." Asking Source to fill every cell of your humanity with turquoise singing light will support you in creating freedom from the inside out. True freedom supports you in receiving what you desire without the urge to run away.

Healing Experience
Freedom Within, Freedom Without

Close your eyes and take a deep and centering breath. Step through the purple door into the emerald garden of your Heart. Find your divine inner child and ask to see your freedom.

An enticing turquoise lake appears, and your divine inner child invites you to take a swim. The lake is clean and lovely. Swim out into the water and as you swim, your body will turn into pure energy. Your divine inner child is swimming with you.

Shake your atoms as if you are a rattle and watch all the old imprisonment stories leave you. These stories include any lives where you or an ancestor lived in slavery of any kind. Any sad stories of financial enslavement or being enslaved by a marriage, relationship, or type of work will also dissolve in the lake.

Once you are free, your energy will rise in vibration and the lake will shimmer with golden fire. The turquoise color will grow brighter, and we ask you to say, "Thank you, Creator, for filling every atom of my humanity with true freedom!"

Your divine inner child will call your full name and you will return to human form. Swim to the shore and rest on the soft emerald ground and soak in the warmth of the Central Sun.

Humanity's last and most sinister deep subconscious motivation is guilt. Guilt can convince a human being that they want what they don't really want. Guilt can make a human being completely forget to ask Source for what they truly want. We share the Truth with you that faith in your innocence seems to be what is lacking. Your Soul is innocent no matter what kind of nightmare your ego has dreamt in this life or any other. We cannot encourage you enough to forgive the nightmares of the past, trust in your evolution, and transform the guilt in your vessel. Because guilt is usually intertwined with the belief that you deserve to suffer and the belief that you deserve to be punished, we say unconditional self-love is lacking. To love yourself, as Mother-Father-God loves you, can be one of the most seemingly impossible things for a human being to do. Please soak in the eternal love we offer you in our next deepest healing experience.

Healing Experience
Undiluted Love for You

Close your eyes and take a gentle breath in and exhale completely. Repeat until you feel safe. As you breathe, we are placing a shawl of pure, white-gold, undiluted love over your shoulders. Our shawl of love melts the emotional burdens, overwhelming responsibilities, and guilt inside of you.

And the shawl grows into a thick and comforting blanket of undiluted love that is soaking into your back, head, arms, and front. As soon as the first blanket soaks into your body, a new blanket replaces it. This repeats until you are totally saturated with undiluted love.

Say, "Thank you, Creator, for filling my humanness with the transforming love of forgiveness. True forgiveness tells me that I am lovable no matter what has happened to me. True forgiveness tells me that I am innocent no matter what I have done. Any harm that I have caused another knowingly or unknowingly, I send to the Central Sun. Thank you, Central Sun, for transforming my guilt into Heart Power."

And we take off the symbolic chains of guilt, suffering, and punishment from your neck, wrists, and ankles and turn them to dust. These are the chains that prevent you from hearing what Soul wants you to have. These are the chains that prevent you from asking the Great Universe to provide for you.

We place a force field of undiluted love around you that will feed love to your cells for all your days. When you consciously remember that it is there and give thanks that it protects you, it will grow ever stronger.

Now that you understand the importance of receiving what is essential to your well-being, it will be easier for you to let Soul support you. We must encourage you to have no fear in asking for what you desire as often as it makes you feel good to ask. God is listening and every one of your prayer requests will be answered in divine timing and in divine order. One simple, yet profound tool helps the Great Universe respond by sending you the energy that will manifest what you need and want. Stay aware of doubt. When you find yourself doubting your Soul, doubting your ability to receive, or doubting the Divine Mother and Divine Father, banish doubt and call Trust into your mind and body.

Healing Experience
Doubt Out, Trust In

Close your eyes and focus on your breathing, taking slow, focused, deep breaths. Step over the threshold of the purple door and look for your divine inner child who is playing in a huge violet-fire fountain of transformation and forgiveness. Step into the fountain and allow the wonderful energy to saturate you.

Continue to breathe deeply and say, "Wherever doubt is hiding within me, I release it and I forgive myself for having doubts. I welcome the Divine Mother and Father of the Great Universe to fill me with Trust."

Watch the color of the fountain change from violet to bright green with gold sparkles. Allow the energy of Trust to permeate the armor of the ego and say, "I trust in me. I trust in Soul. I trust that I am receiving even more abundance than what I ask for from the Great Universe."

Be aware of when the old male has seduced you into a doubting frame of mind. When in doubt, your ego will naturally go into control mode. Control stops the flow of receiving, and the old male gets very excited when he has the chance to keep you risk avoidant and easy to manage.

The Twin Sisters of Intuition and Creativity

Fear's old male teaches you the importance of keeping your mind's frequency tuned to the "undiluted love" channel. On this wavelength, you naturally plug into the receiving power of the Divine Mother of the Great Universe. To bring the energy of Source into the mundane plane of Earth, the ego must connect with two very close friends of your divine inner child. Who are these important friends? The Divine Mother's twin daughters, intuition and creativity. Their combined energy is an elegant river that flows nonstop to ground and materialize the highest vibrational energy coming from the Divine Mother to you. The sisters never leave their mother and when you train your mind to listen to intuition, creative genius can never be lacking. All they ask is that you feel your feelings, release lower vibrational emotions, and trust what your intuition guides you to do.

Saturating your mind with the emerald-gold energy of Trust makes it possible for you to hear your intuition. This also prevents the old male and old female from interfering in the wisdom you are receiving. A simple way to live a meditative life all day every day is to stay aware of your breathing and note if you sigh on the exhale. This is your body's way of communicating that you are anxious or frustrated. To swiftly move into a trusting mind, take some deep breaths while running your hands under water (also helpful for connecting with your feelings). Walking in nature while you say all that you are grateful for can help you ground your intuition, especially if you are trying to solve a problem. And when it is challenging to connect with the divine inner child and the twin sisters, repeat, "I surrender to the loving care of Soul." Doing these simple steps will support you in keeping your vibration high and make it much easier to hear what your inner truth is telling you.

Another helpful tool is to check in with your divine inner child throughout your day. Simply close your eyes, put your hands on your heart, and ask your inner child for confirmation that you are connected. This may come into your mind as a vision or as an affirming feeling. Your divine inner child will alert you when fear's old male and old female are contaminating what is flowing in from the sisters.

Intuition will tell you how to be creative in a way that fills you with the excitement and purpose of Soul. Highest vibrational, Heart happy creativity is fueled with inexhaustible Soul Power. When Soul can express its infinite intelligence, feeling confident and motivated will be your new normal. We still need to warn you that the old male and the old female will try to distract you. Watch out for them sneaking three distracting questions in through the back (subconscious) door. Their questions are predictable and not in any certain order. They will ask, "Will what you hope to create have any value to others?" and hint that it likely will not be what others want. They will ask, "What if what the sisters are saying is wrong?" paired with "What if you never achieve what you need to achieve?" Added to these three favorites of the old male and old female are your own emotional buttons left over from childhood.

Having awareness of your own "booby trap" old male and old female triggers is important! Have you ever been focused on the next step in your creative process, and out of nowhere your mind becomes plagued with negative thoughts? This unwanted and paralyzing mental voice whispers that you are incapable of creating anything of worth. If you grew up in a critical household then the old male and old female will often use the same language that your family members used. Hurtful, condescending self-talk will leave your sensitive ego feeling overwhelmed and defeated. During those times when your ego feels most unworthy, you may feel incapable of hearing or trusting the sisters. Your mind may have an excuse generator that fires out distracting thoughts that offer every possible reason for why you can't be creative. And so, you ask yourself, "Why bother trying in the first place?" When the old male and the old female jump into your mental conversation, it may feel like you are drowning in judging thoughts showing you how insignificant your ability is compared with others. Soon your ego is convinced that you are hopeless, helpless, and in need of a rescue.

We can help you eliminate crashing into the fear that the sisters and their Soul Power have abandoned you to fail and to suffer all alone. Some of you call these emotional triggers and having your buttons pushed "falling down the rabbit hole." To help lift the vibration of your thoughts and feelings when they plummet, we need you to stay aware of the hurts from childhood and transform them. It is impossible for you to not be good enough to receive assistance from your Soul and your team of Helpers in Heaven. From our perspective, your triggers help you to learn that the creativity-stomping ghosts of the past are merely the old male and old female trying to teach you to have faith in yourself. The sisters will tell you they cannot flow at full strength without your having sufficient rest and solitude. In all situations, when you cannot find the sisters, check in and see if you are mentally or physically exhausted and emotionally drained or overwhelmed. If you hear a yes, please try any of the healing experiences to support restful sleep in part 7.

Our first deep healing tool to help you hear the sisters of intuition and creativity is to break out of the negative-parent prison.

THE NEGATIVE PARENT PRISON

The negative parent is the judging, punishing, or "poor me" voice of either parent in your head. This inner voice may tell you to follow in Mom's or Dad's footsteps and to not achieve less or more than they have. A brutal inner voice may tell you that you will never amount to anything and that everything you do is worthless. Whatever the negative parent is saying to you, we say that you do not want to continue to be the same kind of parent to your own divine inner child who is always listening to every thought you think about yourself. No matter how abusive, controlling, judging, and cruel your parents or guardians may have been, none of this treatment was about you. It was about them, and you can now let it go for the greatest good of all concerned. At any time that you become aware of a condescending voice in your mind, leap into our deepest healing exercise and break out of the negative parent (voice) prison.

Healing Experience
Releasing the Negative Parent Voice

Take a deep breath. Say, "I Am ready to feel free!"

Step through the purple door into the safe sanctuary of Heart. Your divine inner child, and your divine parents are waiting for you.

Walk together to the violet-fire river that is just over the hill and step into the soothing energy of Creator's crown chakra.

The river rises above your head, and you can breathe freely in the violet singing light. Your divine-feminine mother and your divine-masculine father gently unzip the energy meridian of your emotional body. This important meridian runs from just above the top of your head to just below your feet.

Proclaim, "I release all neglectful and negative aspects of my parents and childhood caregivers [say their names if you like] into the violet-fire river. I forgive these painful memories. I release all old males and old females who are distracting me and encouraging me to feel inadequate or unworthy. I thank them for this test because I know I am an amazing Creation of God. I release my negative, judging selves into the violet-fire river. Thank you, Soul, for filling me with unconditional love for myself. I choose to forgive myself and to love myself unconditionally!"

See the river turn ruby with emerald sparkles. Say, "Thank you, Divine Mother and Mother Earth for filling me with unconditional love, acceptance, and approval of myself."

See the river turn a rich cobalt blue with turquoise ribbons running through it. Say, "Thank you, Divine Father for filling me with acknowledgment of my true value as a divine being. Thank you for filling me with courage, confidence, and success."

See the river turn into all the colors of the rainbow with gold and silver sparkles. Say, "Thank you, divine inner child for filling me with Trust and faith that I Am a creative force. I Am ready to be happy!"

Step out of the river and lie down on the soft emerald grass. Allow the warmth of the Central Sun to fill you with confidence, self-esteem, and Trust in your worth as a divine human being.

Remember to call on the aid of your Angels to keep your conscious mind aware of your thoughts and feelings. Asking yourself throughout the day, "What do I feel? What do I need? Is there anything that I am afraid to request of the Great Universe?" This will help you stay alert to your emotional triggers—fodder for the old male and old female to distract you from receiving abundance from Source.

The second healing tool Soul uses to lead you is to be aware of what we call the magic parent seduction. We encourage you to pay attention to the vibration of mind and body. If you need a boost in vibration, try saying positive affirmations, writing prayers, meditating, or resting before the old male and old female put you in a state of panic. They may suggest you are hopeless and need a "magic parent" to rescue you. Waiting for magic parents distracts you from listening to your divine inner child and the sisters of intuition and creativity. The sisters open the flow of your receptivity to bringing in wealth from Source. This is the easiest way for you to live a meaningful and abundant life.

THE MAGIC PARENT SEDUCTION

Humanity has been taught to substitute the parental support that you did not have as a child with money, especially when you are seeing yourself as inadequate. When you cannot access the sisters and feel helpless, the old female will encourage you to believe that having lots of money will solve your problems. The old male will bark, nonstop, that a divine rescue is having someone other than yourself show up to take care of you. When this care is financial and costs you your independence, you have fallen for fear's magic-parent trap. Although you may not see it as a trap, when you compromise your goals and dreams and send the sisters into exile, you are also telling the Great Universe that you don't need God's resources.

Where there is a longing for a magic parent to give you lots of money, you can be sure you have a neglected or mistreated child within expecting to be disappointed. Money may be the surrogate parent that you can control; however it is not the source of a jubilant life. Allow us the joy of helping you to transform the disappointment that you have experienced in life by changing the broken, tragic past into a happy childhood today. We invite you to call your divinity into your humanity and experience a newfound spontaneity, exuberance, and trust in your creative pursuits. What does this look like? It looks like no longer spending your energy waiting for someone or something to rescue you.

Below is our list of fantasy scenarios. Review each one and add any of your own that we might have missed. As you read through the list, make note of any fantasy that causes you to feel a reaction in your body and know that this fantasy needs to be released and sent to the Central Sun. Creativity is your pipeline to receiving wealth. Yes, you can receive financial wealth in a multitude of positive ways; however, to wait for it instead of putting your energy into being creative is a waste of your time. Say no to waiting any longer for your fantasy to materialize when there is a much easier way to get what you desire.

▶ Fantasy Scenarios

Don't wait . . .

- To win the lottery, make the perfect gamble or investment so you can do what you truly want to do and live the life you truly want to live
- For the perfect partner who will be the responsible and generous financial provider or the nurturing caregiver who will love you and accept you as you have always needed and wanted to be loved and accepted
- For the promotion or dream job to materialize while in the meantime you suffer at the job you have now
- For an authority figure to value your contribution or genius and place you where you deserve to be placed
- For the friend who will step up and help you because you would step up and help them if you had the resources they have
- To be rescued by anyone who appears to have what you want and more than what they need
- To start, finish, or launch your own creative project because someone needs to support you financially
- To start, finish, or launch your own creative project because you need others' approval
- For the money to "fall from the sky" and materialize so that you can do what makes you happy
- To be discovered and recognized as the gem that you are and

become the adopted princess or prince of the family that will make your dreams come true while you sit and eat cake

Healing Experience
Letting Go of the Magic Parent

Bring to mind the fantasies from the list above that caused a reaction in your body. Close your eyes and take a deep breath and say, "I surrender all fantasies that are limiting the flow of abundance that wants to come to me."

See each fantasy as a book wrapped in gold paper and toss the book into the violet-fire dumpster saying, "I forgive myself in all ways. I release the fantasy, and I send it to the Central Sun to be transformed into confidence and faith in my intuitive and creative ability."

Are you now ready to stop waiting and to ask your Soul to plant some seeds of genius in your creativity garden? We hope your answer is YES! Help the ego recognize the difference between a brilliant idea and an old male one by feeling your feelings and listening to your gut intuition. This helps connect your consciousness with the home of the sisters, the feminine brain. The feminine brain is the fertile soil where viable creative ideas from Heaven plant themselves within you. Being creative in a way that obeys the Law of One—for the greatest good and highest joy of all concerned—opens the vault of the Great Universe. Your financial resources may or may not come directly from the produce grown in your creativity garden; however, when it does, the harvest is endless and changes the world in beautiful ways.

℺Your Creativity Garden

As soon as you ask to receive from the Divine Mother of the Great Universe, you begin to open your creativity. Creativity belongs to the feminine brain. Grounding the sisters' creative genius and intuitive direction streaming into your conscious awareness requires that your feminine mind is open and receptive. Because you will want to plant your seeds of creative genius in fertile soil, we recommend a molecular clearing of the repressed feminine. Please read through the following healing experience. Doing it at bedtime works very well—even if you fall asleep before completion. We will take care of this for you.

ℋealing Experience
Preparation: Clearing Repression of the Feminine

Close your eyes and see the purple door open before you. Just on the other side of the door is a violet-fire ocean of undiluted love. The moon is full, and her light is dancing on the waves.

Your divine feminine and divine inner child appear at the doorway, and each take you by the hand and tug you into the loving energy.

You move effortlessly through the violet ocean and arrive in the middle of a circle of 12 colorful, leaping dolphins—the 12 Archangels in disguise.

Lie down inside of the ruby shell that is open and waiting for you.

The dolphins begin to hum a lullaby that lifts ancient and painful stories from your molecules and atoms.

Say, "I release my female ancestors' stories of repression, abuse, sacrifice, self-denial, guilt, unworthiness, and lost personal power and freedom. I forgive all of it for all of us, even if it is unforgivable."

Rest peacefully in the ruby shell. The violet-fire energy of Creator's crown chakra soaks into the cells of your humanity, traveling down into your DNA. It all feels wonderful!

An emerald singing light appears with the violet. Say, "I release and I forgive the fear and lies that say the feminine and female cannot be trusted. I release and I forgive the belief that to feel my feelings and listen to my intuition is dangerous. I release and I forgive the belief that to receive my living through my creativity is unreliable and unsafe and may lead to exile and starvation. I release and I forgive all the disappointments in life, in people, and in any choice that went against my will or was based on the sacrifice of the will of any of my female ancestors. I release and I forgive the lie that God and men may punish me if I ask for anything in return for my service to God, humankind, and Earth. I forgive especially that which my female ancestors were taught is unforgivable."

And when the sun rises, either in your visualization or when you wake from your sleep, say, "Thank you, Central Sun, for saturating me with love and gratitude for my feminine, my divine feminine, and the Divine Mother of the Great Universe. Thank you, Divine Mother of the Great Universe, through the divine feminine of my Soul, for refueling my clear intuition, creative genius and inspiration, and trust in God."

Your creativity garden can be found within your Heart. Your divine inner child, divine feminine, and divine masculine have been tending it for you. They welcome you to join them in the fun of receiving the seeds from Source, planting the seeds, watching them grow, harvesting the abundance, and sharing the wealth. We say to you that there are many "plants" and "trees" growing in your garden and orchards. The old male and old female will try to tell you that none of them, unless status quo approved, will have any success. Don't let weeds of fear and doubt grow in your garden. How do you do this? Say, "I surrender to the joy, love, and fulfillment of my Soul." We trust that you will put our gardening practices to good use in your daily life, and we encourage you to keep at least one creative project or activity always going. Creativity is the miracle ingredient needed to keep a continuous harvest of abundance coming into your life.

THE 12 ARCHANGELS' GARDENING PRACTICES

Both the ego and Soul will offer seeds to be planted in your creativity garden based on what you need and desire to receive in life. Often, the ego is unaware that its brilliant idea has been downloaded from Soul. To save time in discerning a viable seed from one that will not germinate, ask Soul to give you the seeds to plant in your garden. Now go listen to your divine inner child as they explain to you what each seed represents. You will need to water the seeds with unconditional love, safety, and security from the Divine Mother of the Great Universe. You will need to listen carefully for the clear actions you need to take from the Divine Father of the Great Universe. It is through your divine masculine that your mind will recognize the genius idea that has sprouted.

What do you need to do to nurture this idea so that it grows into a tree that gives delicious fruit? Trust. You will need to ask Soul to fill you with Trust in Source and respect for what you are creating. These two practices—asking to be filled with Trust and asking to be filled with respect for what is manifesting through your efforts—will produce a plentiful harvest to enjoy and to share. Our third practice is to listen to your divine inner child because the direction of the wind can change and your ego must give your creative ideas the freedom to transform, deepen, expand, and manifest as they choose. The physical manifestation may be different from what the ego predicts it to be. Practicing surrender to the Will of your Soul supports you in being the proud farmer who is surprised and humbled by what comes out of the ground.

Healing Experience
Planting Your Creativity Garden

Read through the exercise and then allow your divine inner child and the sisters to guide you through your gardens.

Close your eyes and take a few deep, centering breaths. Walk through the purple door into the emerald meadow of Heart. Your divine inner child, divine feminine and masculine, and the sisters are waiting to greet you.

Follow your helpers into your garden and receive the magic seed from your divine inner child and place it in the fertile earth. Take the watering can from the sisters and shower the seed gently with love from the Divine Mother of the Great Universe (the water that flows from the watering can). Reach up to the sky and pull a ray of Central Sunlight closer to you and to your newly planted seed. Feel the warmth and growing power of the Sun.

Say, "Thank you, seeds of great potential, for one day becoming a tree that bears delicious fruit many will enjoy."

Follow your divine inner child, divine feminine, and divine masculine to the ruby pool of the Divine Mother of the Great Universe and allow your entire being to be saturated with ruby love, safety, and security.

As you are soaking in the ruby waters, ask the sister of intuition to tell you what the creative idea is that has been planted in your garden. Your divine masculine will place a violet hat on your head to help your mind stay clear of doubt. When you know what the planted seed represents, open your eyes and write it down.

If you experience any difficulty in connecting with your intuitive knowing, we recommend that you ask for help from your divine feminine and divine masculine. Please do not push your mind because this will only invite in fear's old male and old female. Instead, go for a walk and focus on putting one foot in front of the other. As you walk, say inside your mind, "I am willing to know, and I choose love." Another tool that you can use is to run your hands under water or take a shower. Focus your attention on the feeling of the water. Say, "I am willing to feel excited and happy about the idea that Soul has given to me." Be patient; trees take time to grow, and we use the metaphor of a fruit tree for a reason. Creative ideas take time to germinate in your mind, and they need time to develop into the project, new vocation, significant life change, or happy childhood that is your destiny to experience. The details and application of your idea will reveal itself when you feel safe emotionally, and your mind is in a peaceful state of surrender. Because your intuitive-feminine mind must connect with your masculine mind for your idea to be translated into clear thought, we encourage you to do a molecular scrub to lift the vibration of your masculine. You will need his help to clearly understand what you need to do going forward.

Healing Experience
Germination: Freeing the Repressed Masculine

With your eyes open, stand up and ask for Archangel Michael of the Central Sun to clear your vessel of the fear of being judged, humiliated, or disrespected or of misusing your will power. Michael will send his sapphire blue Sword of Truth and Awareness down your spine.

Breathe and allow yourself to adjust to the shift in your vibration now that you have Archangel Michael's energy of the highest vibrational truth running up and down your spine.

Close your eyes. Step through the purple door and swim like a powerful fish to the circle of Angels waiting for you in the violet-fire ocean of transformation and forgiveness.

Your divine inner child is waiting for you and takes your hand once you enter the circle.

A brilliant white singing light begins to rise from below your feet and fill your body. Say, "Wherever my masculine is injured, repressed, lost, angry, trapped in guilt and unworthiness, or held in punishment, I release him. I release him for my ancestors. I release him for my past lives. I forgive everything that needs to be forgiven, and I send all his hurt and pain to the Central Sun."

The color changes from white to cobalt blue. Please say, "Wherever I hold the memory of my human male having to lie, compromise his integrity, or force himself to do what is not for his greatest good, I forgive it all. I release it all, and I send all the fear and lies to the Central Sun."

Watch as the ocean changes from violet to turquoise. Ask for your divine masculine, together with the Divine Father of the Great Universe, to restore your human male to the highest vibration of courage, willingness, confidence, strength, and intelligence.

Our next gardening practice will teach you how to best support the growth of your seedling. Seedlings do not appreciate being smothered with worry about their growth and demands for them to bear fruit before they are ready. Waiting is not easy for a human being. The ego wants instant gratification, and it wants to know the future. To support your ego, please remind yourself that once your idea has been planted, Soul will give you the next step in the development of the idea. Until Soul sends the next step to your mental inbox, we suggest that you go play with your divine inner child in the creativity garden of your life. Ask your divine inner child for something that is fun and nurturing in some creative way. This activity, whether mental or physical, will help your life grow and blossom. Once again, we remind you that doing something that is for your highest joy, your greatest good, and the greatest good of all helps you to receive abundance from the Great Universe.

Healing Experience
Playing in the Garden of Your Creative Imagination

We suggest that you read through this experience. Feel free to substitute what feels euphoric and inspiring for your Heart and ego.

Close your eyes, take a few deep breaths, and step through the purple door. Waiting for you is your divine inner child and their dragon. Both are smiling at you.

Your divine inner child introduces you, by name, to three of your guardian Angels. Each Angel also has a magical dragon, and each is a different color of the rainbow.

Your Angels will lift you and your divine inner child onto the back of your dragon. Your first mission is to rescue your unfulfilled dreams from your past. These dreams may be from past lives or ideas that you brushed aside in this life because you could not see the financial value or practicality in developing them.

All the dragons take flight and soar high in the air. What color of singing light is pouring from the dragon's nostrils and mouth? Is there anyone in your life that you would like your dragon to breathe on?

The dragons fly into a mysterious tunnel that takes you back in time. They land on an extinguished star where everything appears to be ash and colorless. The Angels ask that everyone sit comfortably in their saddles. A concert is about to begin!

Your guardian Angels begin to sing. All the dragons begin to beat their tails on the ground, making deep drumming sounds that you can feel in your bones.

The ash begins to move and swirl into the air. A most beautiful palace appears, and through the windows, you can see treasures lighting up in every room. The palace houses your abandoned creative ideas, unfinished projects, and forgotten dreams.

All the dragons begin to breathe rainbow fire onto the palace, and it becomes saturated in the colors of the Central Sun. Treasures start to fly out of the windows and land at the feet of your guardian Angels.

Your Angels and divine inner child sort through the treasures for you and collect what is valuable.

What you need to know about the treasure, you will know, and what is best to remain a mystery will remain a mystery. The Angels and your divine inner child gather all the important treasure dreams that will, indeed, come true and place them in purple sacks on the back of your dragon.

You and your divine inner child are magically transferred to a new dragon, and you sit behind an Angel. Your dragon carries your treasure straight to the Central Sun, and your Angel takes you back to the garden in your Heart.

Once you feel the emerald ground under your feet, hold the hand of your divine inner child, and say, "I call my lost power to me. I call my abandoned creative energy to my garden, recharged with the highest vibrational inspiration!"

Look around your creativity garden with your divine inner child. What new seeds are growing? Say, "Thank you, new and wonderful ideas that will one day bless me with true happiness and lasting fulfillment."

FIRING UP YOUR CREATIVITY TO SUPPORT THE GROWTH OF THE GARDEN

What makes one activity creative and another activity something you do because it must be done? True creativity comes with a leap of faith, something that stretches you into new territory. Real creativity asks that you believe in yourself. If you do not believe in yourself, ask Divine Oneness to fill your humanity with Trust and faith in yourself. Human beings can be afraid to take a risk because they fear judgment, failure, or both. If you are one of these human beings, then put your fear in violet fire and transform it into courage.

Fueling your creativity begins with your willingness to feel your feelings because creativity lives within the feminine part of your brain. Keep asking these two questions that are interrelated: "What is it that I feel? What is it that my feeling is telling me that I need?" Once this becomes second nature to you, it will be effortless to ask, "What is it that Soul is creating through me, right now?" The answer may be as simple as solving a problem, organizing your closet, or writing an email with affection. You are always creating your reality together with your Soul, so it is impossible for you to not be creative. Trusting this to be true helps your creativity garden grow and helps you receive from the Great Universe.

We ask that you think of creativity as water that is flowing from Source through an antique pump—your conscious mind. If your conscious mind is full of the old male and old female's messages that you are not enough and that the sisters of creativity and intuition have no value, then we have a problem. From the ego's perspective, this issue can have you believe that your garden is dead when it is very much alive—the pump simply needs to be primed to help the water flow. Please follow our steps to priming your pump so that your creative genius can flow through you in a way that the ego can acknowledge and keep it flowing.

1. When you cannot hear and have no sense of what idea Soul has planted in your garden, then put your hands or body in water. You can also distract your ego mind by doing some type of physical activity. This can be housework, yard work, running, walking, or swimming. We do not recommend paperwork or competitive sports for priming your creativity pump.

2. Immerse yourself in coral and orange. See these colors of singing light move in a figure-eight pattern, starting at your feet, crossing at your heart, and bending at the top of your head. The top of the number 8 will be at the top of your crown. Say, "Thank you, Soul, for firing up my creative furnace and for helping my conscious mind listen, trust, feel, and recognize the value of the ideas coming forth."

3. Ask your guardian Angels to vacuum your mind with a violet-fire vacuum cleaner. Ask for all not-good-enough thoughts, should thoughts, and negative what-if-something-goes-wrong thoughts to be vacuumed out of your head and sent to the Central Sun.

4. Take a nap if you are tired and as you rest, see yourself wrapped in a coral blanket. If you are hungry, eat something orange or red. Repeat, "I surrender the resistance of my ego to the flow of Soul."

5. If you still feel unclear about what has been planted in your creativity garden, ask your divine inner child and sisters of intuition and creativity to bring you a message through someone else. You will either hear someone tell you your own idea or something close enough that it registers in your mind. If all of this fails to prime your creativity pump, then please repeat the healing experiences to clear the repression of both your feminine (see page 76) and masculine (see page 80).

6. Remind yourself that it is not your responsibility to make your creativity pump work. This is the job of Soul and of your team of Helpers in Heaven. Knowing this can be such a relief on its own that the pump will begin to work, and your creative genius will begin to flow.

Healing Experience
Firing Up Your Creativity

Close your eyes and put your hands on your belly. Take some deep breaths and feel your belly expand into your hands with your in-breath and deflate with your exhale. Repeat until you feel relaxed.

See yourself resting peacefully on a ruby float, drifting on a serene violet-fire lake. The lake is protected by a circle of 12 great crystals, and you can see rainbows being reflected on to the water.

Say, "Unworthy selves, I acknowledge and love you. I now release you into the violet-fire lake to be transformed into worthiness. I Am willing to share my creative efforts!"

Say, "Damaged selves, abused selves, victimized selves, and all selves within me that feel they have no value, I acknowledge you and I love you. I now release you into the violet-fire lake to be transformed into personal power and self-esteem. I invite personal power and confidence to restore me."

Say, "Selves that believe they only fail and rarely succeed, I acknowledge and embrace you. I now send you into the violet-fire lake to be transformed into success. I call my divine birthright to be successful into my humanity."

Say, "Selves that feel hidden, underappreciated, unlovable, and unlucky, I acknowledge and love you. I now release you into the violet-fire lake to be transformed into self-respect and positive acknowledgment. I welcome overflowing respect and positive acknowledgment to strengthen me."

Say, "Ignored children, undervalued children, and disrespected children within, I acknowledge you and I love you. I now ask the 12 Archangels disguised as the crystals to reveal themselves and lift you into the loving arms of Mother-Father-God. I invite the highest magic of Source to restore my creative imagination so that magnificent fruit appears on the trees in my creativity garden."

The violet-fire lake begins to move underneath the ruby raft and bright coral bubbles begin to bubble up on the surface of the water. Catch a bubble with your hands and swallow it. Say, "I allow my creative fire and passion to ignite fully and joyfully."

The violet color of the lake has now transformed into a vibrant golden orange. You can see flashes of ruby, fuchsia, and scarlet dancing beneath the coral bubbles. Call the energy of the lake into your belly and see the creative fire of Soul fill you from the top of your head to your toes.

The energy is now pouring out the top of your head, the palms of your hands, and the soles of your feet. It feels incredible.

Say, "I allow the creative fire and passion of Soul to move me from any story of lack of faith in my creativity into true and lasting respect, confidence, and trust in myself. I give thanks that this is so!"

The ego may want to measure the growth and success of all creative projects, which can make you feel like you are caught in a nettle bush. Obsessing is something the ego does well; however, it can stop your creative flow instantly. Along with obsession, perfectionism is a call to the old male and old female to swiftly invade your garden with doubt, impatience, and frustration when nothing is wrong. Give everything that grows in your garden to the Great Universe so that Divine Oneness can expand what is growing for you. This giving to God and letting it go from the ego supports your Soul's energy of creation and manifestation on Earth to work in unison and in perfect divine order.

Your divine masculine, through your conscious awareness, will identify the fruits of your garden. You will be told, step-by-step, how to ripen the fruit, pick the fruit, and offer the fruit for tasting. The sister of intuition will continue to bring through instructions from your divine feminine on the healthiest way to share your harvest, without compromising your values and integrity. The manifestation of the creative genius of your Soul needs to be shared with others. Many divine ideas need the help of other human beings to transform into a viable business or offering. For example, you find the seed for a remarkable novel growing in your garden. We add to our imaginary story that you have never considered yourself to be a writer. Immediately there is disbelief that this idea could grow into a sapling, let alone a healthy tree that will one day produce edible fruit.

Soul's first step for the ego may be to bring the idea of taking a creative writing class into your mind or your divine inner child might nudge you into a bookstore where you find yourself purchasing a book on how to write and publish your first novel. We wish to reassure you that you will be guided at each step, from receiving the idea to writing the first words, sentences, and paragraphs. As you continue to give your story to Source, you will find that your writing flows much easier and before you know it, you will be ready to publish your manuscript.

Will there be moments when you need to clear the weeds of doubt and fear out of your garden? You can be certain of it. Your awareness and detachment will see the seed of an idea evolve into all that it is destined to be. What makes us, the 12 Archangels, so certain that you will be successful? We have full faith in the mighty power of your Heart to attract to you the help you need. Whether Soul plants a seed for a book or for a business that produces something that benefits Schoolroom Earth, you will need other human beings to add their creative genius to your harvest so it will be of the finest quality. Let your Heart Power surprise you by attracting exactly what you need into your reality, and the people who can be the most beneficial in supporting your creative expression. The sisters, together with Heart Power, will direct you to find collaborators who have already mastered what you choose not to do yourself. This allows you to use your time and energy efficiently and confidently.

Cultivating with Heart Power

Your Soul wants your ego to be happy. A happy ego, aligning with Heart and Soul, is a person who is a singing ray of the Central Sun. Such a human being asks Source for everything they desire. They receive it because they have the patience to wait for all things to come to them in divine order. This human being wisely fills up with Trust and walks in faith that they are always loved and cared for no matter the situation. They are rarely miserable because they accept that they are on Earth to work with the greatest Power of undiluted love in all aspects of life. You have our full support and encouragement to be this person. We acknowledge your courage and remind you that you deserve to experience a safe, secure, happy, and wealthy childhood for all your days. This has always been Mother-Father-God's plan for you. Now is the time for you to use the energy of the ego to focus on being grateful for who you have become even if you have not arrived at the goal. Gratitude is the mental frame of mind that will support you in experiencing the very best results of the law, As Above, So Below and As Within, So Without. You were born with the ability to draw to you all the highest vibrational support you need. Do you agree that the most successful farmer has great help and the best weather?

We fully acknowledge that not all creative activities need to be seen, symbolically, as a fruit tree that expands into an orchard. The sisters may also provide ideas that focus on fun. Enjoyable activities that encourage the expression of your creative passion help you receive from Source. As you spend time in your creativity garden, Soul may send you an exciting idea that will allow you to receive your paycheck from Mother-Father-God. If you do not need to earn a livelihood because you are set financially, then Soul will send you inspiration on how you can be a consciousness shifter and participate in higher service to Schoolroom Earth. Why? Because of the second divine law, the Law of One. When you do something that is for your greatest good and highest joy and for the greatest good of all, life can only get better. Using Heart Power, through the third divine law, to draw to you the help you need to transform your creative idea into a service that benefits others will ensure your success. Heart Power attraction is not something you can buy no matter how much money you may have to spend. It is something that Creator gives to you as you raise your vibration and open your life to trusting Soul.

Heart Power attraction is simply all three divine laws working in unison on your behalf, together with your ego actively engaged using positive intention. You can see how your Heart Power attraction is working in your everyday life by being aware of what you are already drawing into your reality. For example, if you need support to launch a new business and your next-door neighbor rings your doorbell and offers to make an impressive website for you, then you can see that your Heart Power attraction is working very well. On the other hand, if you are asking for help and no one is available then this tells you that your Heart Power attracting needs a boost from Soul. Remembering that the outside reflects the inside can be helpful in recognizing if your Heart attraction is working at full Soul Power.

On Schoolroom Earth, part of your education requires that you engage with other human beings. Those people who are completely self-sufficient and avoid having any kind of interaction with other people can be sure that in a future life they will have a physical dependency where they must ask and receive help from others. People who fear human interaction have turned off the Heart Power attraction to protect themselves emotionally. Most human beings' Heart Power can benefit from eight essential healing techniques. You need these tools to assist you in transforming the grief, sorrow, and loss from the past. Grief clogs the human pulmonary system (the heart and lungs) as well as the flow of Heart Power. Please read through the exercise and visualize the steps as you go along. This is a profoundly healing experience and may make you feel physically drained temporarily due to the great release of sorrow. Give yourself time to rest and trust that your energy will return with the intake of joy from Soul. Please do not skip over this step because it is crucial to awakening and expanding your Heart Power attraction.

Healing Experience
Transforming Your Heartache

Breathe in deeply and exhale completely. Walk through the purple door. Join your divine inner child, divine feminine, and divine masculine who you will find standing in a shallow lake, under a white-gold waterfall of pure, undiluted love. Welcome your ancestors to join you under the beautiful waterfall. Say to them, "Thank you, ancestors from my mother's side, father's side, and all my past lives, for participating in the transformation of grief, sorrow, and loss that I carry for you."

Invite all your hurting selves, emotionally, mentally, and psychically overwhelmed selves, and heartbroken selves from this life to join you and your ancestors in the white-gold lake of undiluted love. Begin to chant softly, "I forgive it all. I forgive it for all of us."

As you say the mantra, the waterfall turns violet with the energy of transformation and forgiveness. Open your rib cage as if it is a magic door. Ask your ancestors, divine Self, and hurting human selves to open their heart doors as you have done.

Say, "Grief, I acknowledge you. Loss, I acknowledge you. Sorrow and overwhelm, I acknowledge you. I release you into the violet-fire waterfall of forgiveness and ask that you return to the Central Sun to be transformed into abundant joy."

Listen as your ancestors, divine Self, and suffering human selves acknowledge all that needs to be acknowledged. A great wave of dark energy that tastes like salty tears and cries out as it is released, leaves each participant. Your divine inner child is releasing for your wounded child, your divine feminine is releasing for your human female, and your divine masculine is releasing for your human male.

Once the darkness lifts, the waterfall and lake turn opalescent, sparkling with gold and silver. The sky fills with the white-gold radiance of the Central Sun.

Say together, "I call my joy and trust in a happier life into my humanity!" Repeat until you feel light and free. Thank your ancestors and see them ascend on a white marble staircase to Heaven. See yourself step back through the purple door and then continue reading to discover some helpful tools for activating your Heart Power.

EIGHT DAILY TOOLS FOR HEART POWER ACTIVATION AND EXPANSION

We have eight tools to help you maximize the positive force of your Heart Power. The first Heart Power activation and expansion technique is to practice awareness of what you are drawing to you in the movie of your life and to use the Law of As Above, So Below, As Within, So Without, to change what is happening. For example, if you have a restaurant server who is in a bad mood then ask for any self with a bad mood within you to climb into a ruby canoe and paddle down the violet-fire river to the Central Sun. Shower yourself and the server with Divine Mother's love and watch the outer reality change to mirror what is now expanded within you. The mood of your restaurant server will improve, or they will disappear and be replaced by someone new. This technique also works very well if you find that others are not listening to you or understanding what you are saying to them. Take a moment and listen to your divine inner child and find out what you are not hearing. Doing this will quickly change the outer reality to match the inner, and you will be seen, heard, and understood.

Heart Power is always working and the more aware you stay, the quicker you can shift the movie you are living. Our last example is about those who are super giving. Would you enjoy attracting more people like yourself than those who deplete your energy? When you become aware that you are in the presence of demanding people with empty emotional buckets, then ask Source to flood your entire being with undiluted love until you feel like you are a love geyser. Not only will everyone feel better, but you will also stop attracting people into your personal space who want you to fill them up when what they really need is to plug into Source for themselves. Expanding your Heart Power happens organically when you stay connected with what you are experiencing in your reality and refuse to be a victim of it. Instead, ask the question, "What is this experience showing me about myself?" Shift your vibration with love and change your outer experiences with others by changing your inner experience with yourself.

The second Heart Power expansion practice is to forgive yourself and all those who have hurt you or disappointed you in the past. Forgiveness activates and expands Heart Power. If you are hurting yourself then you may attract others who are hurt or others who may disrespect you in some way. Therefore, it is important to practice our first tool of staying aware of what you are already attracting into your life, especially when you have asked the Divine Mother of the Great Universe to receive something specific. Please give yourself the gift by letting go of old hurts, resentments, and mistakes and forgive them completely. Forgiveness, especially of yourself, helps you to attract the reliable support you need at the highest vibration of thoughtfulness and respect.

The third Heart Power practice is to accept that you are a divine child of the Great Universe and therefore worthy of giving yourself unconditional approval, respect, and acceptance. By filling up with unconditional love for your human self and by thanking Divine Oneness for you throughout the day, your Heart Power will expand. Heart Power comes from your divine inner child. The more your ego surrenders to listening to this wise sage, the faster you will draw into your life exactly what you need.

The fourth Heart Power expansion tool that increases Heart Power energy and the speed at which it manifests is gratitude. Giving thanks for your creative ideas and each step to develop these ideas will bring support and success into your life. Instead of throwing in the towel when a gardening challenge comes along, thank the challenge as it is your teacher. You can be certain that your tree will produce even better tasting fruit now that you have learned what to adjust either within the project or within yourself or both. Gratitude for the Angels, Helpers in Heaven, your higher Self, the challenges, and even your ego helps Heart Power to expand its reach.

The fifth Heart Power liberation technique is to stay mindful of any limiting or punishing religious beliefs that may block or slow down Heart Power. Having a subconscious or conscious level belief that you are unworthy to receive from others and from God constricts Heart Power. A belief that can be joined with this one is the fear of being punished for asking for help (even if you pay for it). Some religious doctrines encourage suffering as a form of purification and if this belief is activated, you may find it difficult to receive the help you need or the success you have earned. Experiencing lack, or less support than what you need, can be seen by the subconscious as the perfect form of suffering that will purify you. When Heart Power is lacking, do the following, even if you have already cleared suffering, sacrifice, and unworthiness to receive. Place the books (beliefs) in purple boxes and deposit them into the violet-fire river to be transformed. Any trapped fear flows back to the Central Sun and will return to you as clear Heart Power.

Our sixth Heart Power tool is to stop putting pressure on what is growing if it is not growing as fast as you want it to grow. Your divine inner child may have a different vision of what an abundant garden and potential harvest look like when compared with what the ego expects. Pressure from the ego only causes anxiety, which quickly diminishes the Heart Power available for growing the finest produce. When you feel under pressure—time pressure, financial pressure, wounded-self pressure, or external pressure—say, "I send this pressure to the Central Sun. I surrender all of my worries to the care of Soul." Take deep breaths until you feel calm again.

Our seventh Heart Power activation tool is to switch the focus of any fearful or negative thoughts to thoughts of love. Choosing love will fire up your Heart Power and have you feeling hopeful immediately. When fear's old male and old female have crept into your garden and have sown weeds of doubt, choose love. When they bring in the petulance of procrastination, choose love. And when they fill the ego with the desire to be rescued by a magic parent, choose love. Step through the purple door and visualize a shower of rainbow love falling on your garden and all that is growing. Breathe in the expansiveness of undiluted love and ask Soul to fill you with trust in you and your produce and faith that you are a divine child of God.

Our eighth Heart Power opening technique is to pay attention to when you are feeling guilty about having fun, being creative, enjoying life, and taking good care of yourself. Guilt zaps Heart Power and will make you feel less confident about reaching your potential. All the help that you need to take the seed of creative genius through its development into a tree that bears delectable fruit will come to you. The help to harvest the fruit, market the fruit, and deliver the fruit to those who will benefit will come to you. Heart Power will attract the people, resources, and opportunities that you need to succeed in a way that will feel expansive and joyful. This happens organically, without force or control.

Healing Experience
Activating Heart Power

Close your eyes and focus on your breathing until your mind is quiet. Step through the purple door and look at the flowering fruit trees. Smell their fragrance and thank them for their beauty, scent, and overflowing potential that they share.

Together with your divine inner child, divine feminine, and divine masculine, gather the books that you discover at the base of the trees and toss them into the big violet-fire dumpster in the middle of the orchard. These books represent limiting beliefs that tell you that you are not allowed to be successful or have your dreams come true or enjoy the freedoms that you desire.

As you put the books in the dumpster, say, "I release. I forgive. I allow my Heart to draw to me all I need to live in Heaven here on Earth."

Your divine masculine hands you a gold shovel and instructs you to dig around the roots of each blossoming fruit tree. Here you will find smaller books that you do not want to touch. Your divine masculine and divine feminine will take the books from the earth and place them on the sapphire blue coals of highest Truth that line the bottom of the violet-fire dumpster. These books represent the lies that tell you that you are guilty for being born, that you are too unworthy to ask Source for what you need, and that you are unlovable. There may be an occasional book that describes how you will always be a loser and that life on Earth will always be a constant struggle. All beliefs based on lies and full of fear will be placed in the dumpster. Again, say, "I release all of the lies that limit my receiving. I forgive all the lies. I allow my Heart to draw to me all I need to live as Creator's happy, safe, and unencumbered child."

Your divine inner child asks you to climb the huge oak tree in the middle of the orchard. Please choose a branch and sit together.

Your divine inner child will smile a knowing smile and place their hands on your heart and ask you to take a deep breath. Everything turns emerald with gold sparkles. All you feel is undiluted love and trust in Soul. In this moment, let go of everything and everyone that the ego believes you need to succeed. Say, "I surrender everything to the direction and care of my Soul and my team of Helpers in Heaven."

Your team of Helpers in Heaven are sitting in the upper branches of a huge Oak. We hear everything you wish to communicate. What does your Heart want to say? What is lacking in the movie of your life? Share what is lacking with us. We say that we already know and for you to voice it opens your will and expands your Heart Power.

And if your ego will allow, say, "I release my pictures of what wealth looks like to me. I allow myself to receive far more than what I think I want. I allow myself to be the child who is loved, cared for, and lacking absolutely nothing!"

Harvesting
Your Garden

Before you decide on how you will bring your creative efforts into the mundane world, fill up with abundant gratitude for your garden. Give thanks for every idea and inspiration. Give thanks for all the help from both Heaven and Earth that has stepped into your life to support the manifestation of your project. Your creative expression and willingness to allow your pursuits to come to fruition are sources of eternal riches, flowing from the Great Universe, through Soul, to you. We repeat this to take the pressure off your ego. The ego believes that it must be in the know and in control. Control will greatly limit both what you can harvest and how you market the harvest. Knowing what to harvest begins with asking yourself the question, "What do I want?" Asking the question may set off fear's old male and old female's "not good enough" alarm. Flooding your garden with violet fire, before you plan to harvest it, is a very good idea.

Harvesting your garden requires letting go of what did or did not happen in the past because what is ripe for harvest belongs to the here and now. Because your divine masculine is the highest vibration of your ego mind, it is important to ask your divine masculine to translate your intuition (divine feminine) into accurate words and feelings. You can also ask to speak directly to the twin sisters, and your divine masculine will put their directions clearly in your mind. Keeping the vibration of your intuitive feelings and impressions positive helps your ego stay grounded. It also helps the ego to be centered with your Heart and able to focus on taking one step forward at a time.

The greatest challenge that you will have with what to do with your harvest is managing the expectations of the ego. Soul will use your expectations as a plunger to pull up fear from the subconscious layers. We will give you a Schoolroom Earth example to help you understand this phenomenal evolutionary process. Let's say that you are an inventor and you have invented a new technology to help the planet. In your mind, you have complete confidence that your new technology is brilliant and divinely sent. Before even considering asking your higher Self what to do next, the ego is convinced that what you need most is money from investors. When you approach investors, they respond by asking you how much money your invention has made so far. They do not show much interest in the actual potential of your invention and due to their rejection, you tumble down into the trap of the old female and old male.

In our pretend story, this ego did not use Heart Power to bring into reality the help needed, which is not money. This ego did not ask their divine inner child for advice as to what they need to share their invention with the world. This ego did not remember that vibration is everything. What this ego needs to do is to give their invention to the Great Universe and be patient for the sisters of intuition and creativity to reveal the next step. The ego wants instant gratification and the ego looks to the outside world for the solution instead of going within to Source. While practicing patience, this ego would benefit from asking their divine inner child to connect with the Divine Mother and receive into their reality the person who can unlock the next door for them. The door will open, without force, when the door is ready to open. Step-by-step, as the doors open, the invention will find its way into the world. You may ask, "But what about the money? Doesn't this inventor need lots of money to make this happen?" We say that the inventor does not need money until money comes into the story. When money is needed, Divine Oneness will send it to the inventor. When the ego pushes and insists, often you end up feeling enslaved, used, and cheated. Harvesting your garden requires trust, patience, intuition, and perfect timing.

Learn to surrender and trust that nothing you create is by yourself. Divine Oneness is responsible for supporting your creativity and helping your ego evolve. Your evolution is very much an asset because as you evolve, life gets easier and more fluid. What the ego sees as mistakes, Soul sees as learning opportunities, and what the ego sees as rejection, Soul sees as the ego learning trust and patience. What the ego sees as an empty harvest, Soul sees as valuable learning and redirection. We say that a wise ego never gives up. You do need to learn to surrender to Soul and allow the "something unexpected and even better" to appear in your garden. What can you do to help your ego when it is obsessing over what has not happened that you expected to happen? And what can you do to help the ego when the path forward, which appeared so clear, seems to have run into a roadblock?

Healing Experience
Rescuing the Ego

Ask your divine inner child to place a velvet violet-fire hat, lined with emerald silk, on your head. The hat may be as stylish as you wish it to be. We suggest that you allow your divine inner child to be the hat designer. Say, "I let go of the control, frustration, guilt, and anxiety in my mind and vessel. I release all of it, even if I don't want to release it. I forgive myself for anytime I have felt abandoned and let down by Mother-Father-God."

Step through the purple door and lie down on the ruby sofa that is sitting in the middle of a lush garden in full bloom. Ask your divine inner child to bring you the sisters of intuition and creativity. Say, "What is it that I need to learn from my unmet expectations? Can you help me to understand why what is happening obeys the divine laws and, therefore, must be for my greatest good?" The sisters will repeat the answer until you have it, and the truth of the answer feels unshakable.

Get up off the sofa and walk into your creativity garden. Thank every living seedling and tree as well as the fruit on the trees for providing you with all you need to thrive on Schoolroom Earth. Repeat, "I am grateful" until a peaceful determination fills your body, and you know that you are ready to surrender your future to the direction of Soul.

Before you exit the creativity garden, ask your divine inner child to take you to the bright green and sparkling golden waterfall. Stand together and fill up with Trust. Trust is the golden nectar that helps the ego let go of control so you can take the leap of faith into the unexpected. Receiving abundance in a continuous flow asks you to trust more each day.

A question to ask your divine inner child is, "Are we ready to share the first harvest of our creative expression with others?" The old male and old female may hint that your fruit will never ripen. However, when your Heart Power attracts the first customer then share the fruit. And while they are tasting the fruit, fill up with gratitude for the undiluted love that once began as a seed and now benefits another. Your harvest grows when you learn to appreciate what has come through you as the divine essence of Source. It can be difficult for the artist and "genius of quite a lot" to detach their self-worth from what has originated from Creator. Lack of self-esteem and the fear of rejection can be transformed by asking Soul to fill you with awareness of your divinity. Being your true authentic self in the movie of your life helps you experience the success you desire.

We are ready to teach you how to create a new financial reality, even if financial hardship, real or imagined, has never been part of your life's movie. Human beings have sacrificed their creative callings for too long all for the sake of having "financial security." We say to you that this is all a lie designed to make you obey and hand over your power and your treasure to those who can control you with fear's old male and old female conditioning. We invite you to break free and step out of an archaic illusion. As you break free, Soul's singing light expands and reaches further into the darkness that cries out for Truth and freedom. After all, beloved one, you are a mirror of the Central Sun.

PART 4

Creating a New Financial Reality

Mother-Father-God knows the way to bring you what you need. Always having your needs met in the highest vibrational way works far better than only having lots of money.

THE 12 ARCHANGELS OF THE CENTRAL SUN

The Divine Laws
and Money

We invite you to experience the miracle making that happens by simply holding the intention that all currency, in any form, comes from Divine Oneness. Intending that money comes from Source immediately raises the vibration of the thoughtform of money and helps you to receive it through the Divine Mother of the Great Universe. She knows how to support you, and she knows how to give you the security you seek as a Soul living as a human being on Schoolroom Earth. The ancient thoughtform of exchanging currency for a service or product is an old male invention. We believe it is time to change the "hands" of money and toss your wrist and ankle shackles of enslavement into the violet-fire trash bin. When you think you need money, go deeper inside and ask, "What do I truly need?" A simple way to figure this out is to ask yourself, "What am I going to do with the money once I have it?" Are you going to spend it? Save it for an emergency? Share it generously with others? Hoard it because it's all you've got to count on? Reject the money?

Let's start with the highest vibrational spending. When you know what you are going to buy with the money then ask the Great Universe, Mother-Father-God, Creator, and Soul to provide you with what you desire. We will use the example of a new automobile. Purchasing a new car on the outside tells you that you want to move through life in a new way on the inside. When you say, "Soul, I am ready to move through life in a new way. Thank you for providing me with a new vehicle." And feel free to tell Soul the car of your dreams. If Soul agrees with you, then your Soul and Helpers in Heaven will make sure that you have the resources you need to purchase a new car. You can help Soul by asking Source to fill you with freedom and the worthiness to receive your dream car. By working with the Law of As Above, So Below, As Within, So Without, you make it much easier for Creator to send you the funds, which may come as a miraculous surprise to you.

The Law of Energy says that saving money for an emergency lowers the vibration of your energy because it is founded on fear. We understand that every human being feels more comfortable in their skin if they know they will always have food, clothing, shelter, health care, and transportation. We encourage you to go high vibe and say, "Thank you, Divine Mother, for filling every cell of my humanity with your emotional security and physical safety." By starting with "thank you," you are using gratitude, a quality of undiluted love that raises the vibration of your energy to the highest frequency of the Central Sun. By asking to be filled with Divine Mother's safety and security, you are activating your Heart Power to receive from Source through the mundane plane of Earth. Are you ready to take fear out of saving for a rainy day so that you trust you will always have what you need, when you need it? If your answer is yes, then thank the Divine Mother of the Great Universe for filling you with emotional security and physical safety. Also, thank her for providing the help and financial resources you need, arriving in perfect divine timing. Receiving the cash flow you need for a tough spot, money drought, or emergency will always come to you, maybe not in the way the ego expects, but it will come.

Sharing your money generously with others activates the Law of One and is a wise practice. We add that the sharing makes you feel happy and not depleted. When you forgive a financial debt, share because you love to share, and practice generosity, then you are working with all three divine laws, and your financial resources will increase. If you start off with more than enough, you will find that you cannot deplete your reserves below what you need to feel secure. Giving is what Mother-Father-God and Mother Earth do constantly and for you to share your prosperity will only invite in more abundance.

Hoarding money is for the very emotionally poor. Even if these individuals have more money than they can spend in ten lifetimes on Schoolroom Earth, they still feel unsafe deep within themselves. This insecurity is mirrored with feeling threatened that they may lose their money or that they may not have enough if they share it. It exposes a lack of trust in Soul and Divine Oneness. The person who hoards their money is trying to replace the love and care of one or both parents with something that they can control. We ask that you do not judge such a person but that you have compassion for them. Because their wounded self is trying to ignore all three divine laws, they will need to return to Schoolroom Earth until they choose love over fear. We hope that you can see that you will never benefit from holding on to money like it has more value than happiness, loving relationships, and health. From our perspective, you have been conditioned by fear to believe that money is God and that the money god can grant you freedom from a miserable life. Asking the Great Universe to bless you with financial freedom will not give you freedom from anxiety unless you respect the value of undiluted love. Ask Mother-Father-God to fill you with a deep inner security that you will always be well provided for and celebrate the peace that becomes your life.

Repelling financial abundance that is trying to come to you from Source is a familiar story to us. We work endlessly to help you to accept ease with money instead of energetically blocking or rejecting resources because your subconscious tells you that you are in danger. Sometimes it is not just the subconscious but also the ego that can feel unsafe when receiving money. When there has been trauma related to asking for money, receiving money, borrowing money, investing money, or earning money, it can create a significant lack of trust in your relationship with money. It may be easier to live "hand to mouth" to avoid punishment, humiliation, and pain. We offer a healing exercise to lift this trauma out of all those who suffer with it. The transforming energy in the next healing experience will continue to work until the past has been forgiven.

Healing Experience
Clearing Financial Trauma and Suffering

Close your eyes. Take in a deep breath and exhale completely. When you feel centered, walk through the purple door and look to your left for the stairs going down into a dark basement, which is symbolic of your subconscious.

Archangel Gabriel will be waiting for you at the top of the stairs. Gabriel gives you and your divine inner child a lantern with a violet flame and places a force field of many colors around you.

As you start to walk down the stairs, you begin to hear cries for help from people locked in prison cells in the basement. They are symbolic of the lack of trust and faith in your safety to receive money and help. Some represent memories of humiliation of being ridiculed for needing assistance or for being impoverished in a past life. Some of the voices belong to your ancestors who struggled due to war ravishing their lives.

Call out to the voices, "We hear you! We have come to set you free from your suffering, anger, guilt, and shame."

Gabriel, together with your divine inner child, blows into the violet flame of the lantern, and it fills the basement and every jail cell with violet sparkles that grow and expand. The imprisoned catch violet sparks and swallow them. Each one says, "I forgive my guilt and shame, even if it feels unforgivable to forgive. I forgive those who have hurt me. I forgive those who have knowingly taken advantage of me. I forgive it all, and I give the fear and heartache to the Central Sun!"

The wounded begin to dissolve in the violet fire of forgiveness. The flame in your lantern turns a brilliant coral, the color of Soul's creative power. Bookshelves that tower up the walls of the basement start to come into focus. The underground cavern has grown into the size of a cathedral.

Archangel Michael appears and together with your divine feminine and masculine takes the books off the shelves that hold the proof of why it is not safe for you to ask for money when it is owed. They also remove the books that prove it is unsafe to desire financial miracles and relief to come to you.

Other books contain the stories of the secret divisions of those who are not allowed to have money, comforts, and financial security and those who always get what they want and more. A large book tells the lie that those who have more money are superior to those who have less. It is time to let Archangel Michael take all the books to the Central Sun for transformation.

Say, "I release the old lies that bind me to lack, guilt, poverty, servitude, sacrifice, unworthiness, and hardship. I forgive these old stories for all concerned, and I give them to Creator."

The ceiling of the cathedral-sized cavern opens, and rays of the Central Sun pour into the space. You are lifted into the sky and placed on emerald ground.

You see before you a writing desk with a pen and paper. Please watch what magically appears on the paper as Soul writes down all that you truly wish to receive that you never thought was possible. Breathe and say, "I surrender to the abundant prosperity of my Soul. I allow myself to receive all that Soul desires for me. I agree to let go of the fear of not having money and the control of where the money will come from. I surrender all to Soul."

Now, that you are open to receiving the money coming to you from the Great Universe, we wish to share the Truth about money with you. Money does not have the same frequency as the divine laws, which were founded in undiluted love. By honoring the teachings and boundaries of the divine laws, it can appear difficult to manifest the much lower vibrational thoughtform of money. We will help you to transform the sorrow that this vibrational distance may have caused you in this life or in another. Your Heart Power has the attractive force to call money directly to you and to transform its vibration on the way into your wallet and bank account. There are many on your planet that would prefer that you never figure this out because they feel their power comes from fear and not from love. Working with the power of love to transform the thoughtform of money changes financial hardship and anxiety for you and for all those who suffer from financial lack on Schoolroom Earth. We thank you for helping us change the reality of money, currency, credit and debit cards, stocks, and investments. Bank loans, credit card debt, and everything else connected with the exchange of money on Schoolroom Earth can be transformed into a higher vibration!

As you live a creative life and share what grows in your creativity garden, you raise the frequency of the thoughtform of money. The thoughtform of money is deeply contaminated with fear, and all the qualities of the old male and old female. Changing the reality of money is re-creating it from the inside of you. As you do this, money will evolve and become far more accessible to those who will benefit from having it. One day, money will grow out of fashion on Schoolroom Earth because humanity will remember that they are God's Children and able to manifest without the thoughtform of money being needed. For now, we need to teach you how to re-create your own self-worth so that money rises to your frequency of love, making it far easier for you to receive it for being a loving, creative, and giving divine Child of the Great Universe.

Transforming the Fear Held within the Thoughtform of Money

The eighth chakra of protection and purification is the battery of spiritual energy located in a space above your head. One of the roles of this elevated chakra is to connect your superconscious mind with your conscious mind. Held within the white fire of the eighth chakra is a mysterious black box that contains the story (belief paradigms) of the thoughtform of money. This box is full of information including the origins, movement, and manipulation of currency and the secrets, lies, and power plays surrounding it. Although it may be tempting to open the box and see if there is any useful information that may give you the tools to produce and multiply money, we recommend that you keep this box closed. In Truth, we encourage you to keep it locked and request that your higher Self send it to the Central Sun at least once per day. Say, "Thank you, Soul, my higher Self, for sending the black box to the Central Sun. I choose love, and I choose to receive the highest vibrational wealth that is for the greatest good of all."

Where does the black box come from? A long time ago on your planet, a community of egos grew very disconnected from their Souls, or so their egos believed, and they created the thoughtform of currency.

Currency was originally invented as a clever method to cheat and steal by giving insignificant bits of metal or stone in exchange for valuable goods. The idea was a success, and the money thoughtform materialized as currency. With the invention of currency, borrowing and indebtedness soon became common place on Schoolroom Earth. Over time, more of fear's old male and old female's control, intimidation, judgment, greed, unworthiness, resentment, guilt, and punishment were infused into the thoughtform of money.

Mystics, shamans, healers, and seekers of Truth would discover that having money caused fighting and mistrust among friends and so they wanted nothing to do with money and chose to carry and keep only what was minimally necessary. Times have changed and even the wisest and most spiritually awake need money to function in daily life. Spiritual service is expected to be free or to cost very little. If world servers and those who Souls feel called to help Earth are held in survival mode, then they may remain distracted from discovering the dark truth about money. If healers and world servers knew they could use Heart Power to call abundance as needed, they could use their energy, focus, and skill to transform the money thoughtform. Doing this would rapidly change the global story of fear and control witnessed by the One Human Body. Those who invented currency in the first place have become addicted to the power it gives them, and they prefer to keep the simple truth that love transforms the fear embedded in money a secret not to be shared.

As love does its work, money becomes more available to those who will use it for the greatest good of all, at the highest vibration of undiluted love. We repeat, ask Source to give to you what you need and desire instead of asking for money. The money you need will come; however it will be lifted in vibration to meet your own frequency. When you choose to work with the divine laws to earn your living, you help change the reality of money for the greatest good of all.

A question that you might ask us, the 12 Archangels, is "Why do we continue to have money's black box if we have sent it to the Central Sun for transformation?" We share with you that whenever you have despair or frustration about money, especially when you feel hopeless about earning more than what you currently earn, you immediately bring the black box right back to you. Each time that you send it to the Central Sun, you do increase your immunity to the fear that permeates money. Fear multiplies and love transforms. Each time you choose love, you rein in how much the fear in the black box can manipulate you.

Along with the black box that sits in your eighth chakra there are other fear-based beliefs that need to be released for you to positively change your relationship with money. Think of these fear-based beliefs as puppet strings attached to the black box that the old male and old female use to control you and distract you from being creative and from feeling peaceful and safe. These puppet strings have the negative potential to hold you in fear for your survival. They control you so that you're afraid to take a risk and say goodbye to work and relationships that you know lower your vibration.

To keep things simple, we will describe four "puppet strings" of fear that make it possible for you to fall asleep and hand your power over to the old female and old male. Metaphorically, two of the strings control your head and neck, and the other two manipulate your arms and legs. Your head and neck symbolize your courage to respect your integrity as a divine being. They represent your willingness to choose happiness and freedom over self-compromise, and your acceptance of your value to God. Your arms symbolize what you are willing to release and hand over to Divine Oneness. They represent what you are willing to receive from Source. Your legs symbolize the willingness to change directions and walk a new path for your greatest good and highest joy. Being aware of when your self-worth plummets or when you doubt your decisions helps you to recognize when the puppet strings are pulled. Although we don't recommend that you open the black box because it may be all-consuming, we do encourage you to have full knowledge of the four puppet strings and to always carry your sapphire-flame scissors. The contents of the black box have no way to influence you without these strings of attachment that can pull you down.

The first string is the old female's ability to make you think that you are poor and helpless to change your financial situation. Interwoven with the first string, the second string may convince you that you are trapped in the same financial story as your relatives and ancestors. The second string tells you that you are a victim of your upbringing, environment, and education (or lack thereof). The old female uses these two attachments to seduce you into her sticky spider web of unworthiness and self-doubt, physical illness, addiction, or depression. The old female is an expert at slowing you down, pulling your mind and energy away from your creative pursuits, and gradually degrading your self-esteem until you relinquish control to the old male.

The third string is the old male's conviction that you do not have any power when it comes to changing your financial situation unless you work for the old male-saturated patriarchy. This may look like climbing the corporate or military ladder or sticking with work that is predictable, mostly reliable, and comfortable, even if it makes you miserable. When yanked, the old male's puppet strings will have you running back to the safe, familiar, and risk-free way to live your life, even if this is killing you. Your nose will be held to the grindstone, and you will be too afraid to leave a job no matter how unhappy or confining it makes you feel. The fourth string is the fear that you will be abandoned, homeless, bereft, and publicly humiliated for losing control over the source of your money. Controlling money is the same as trying to control your energy. You can stay aware of the vibration of your energy, and you can stay aware of when you need to receive from the Great Universe, but controlling money will only make you obsess over it and before very long, it will likely have control over you and your life. Money is a very poor substitute for Divine Oneness because Divine Oneness can keep you in wealth, no matter what may be in your bank account. Controlling your money automatically puts you in lack because money is laden with fear.

How do you know if fear has tricked you into being afraid of having money, not having it, or having more than enough of it in the future? The answer is simple: because you will be worrying about money or obsessively trying to control money instead of focusing on what is growing and ready to harvest.

Healing Experience
Releasing the Puppet Strings of Attachment to Money

With your eyes open, focus your attention on four imaginary strings hanging down from a black box located about a foot above your head.

Lift your divine inner child up onto your shoulders. Your divine inner child is wearing one sapphire flame glove and one violet-fire glove. Gloves are symbolic for God's undiluted love. Thank your personal superhero for grabbing the four strings and throwing them, black box and all, to the Central Sun. Angels stand watch to make sure that the puppet strings and box are destroyed and transformed into new self-worth for you.

Shower your divine inner child with affection and gratitude. Only the divine inner child has the Heart Power to do the work that needs to be done when it comes to transforming the fear in the thoughtform of money.

Another method that fear's old male and old female use to steal your self-esteem and make you a prisoner is debt. All financial debt with emotional attachment is symbolic of doubt. Financial debt is the mirror of the doubt of self, doubt of Soul, doubt of Creator, and doubt of your value. Financial debts need to be dissolved in the violet-fire ocean of transformation and forgiveness so they disappear. How is this possible? Through faith in the Power of undiluted love and calling on the divine Law of As Above, So Below. You will never owe anything to Source because you are already infinitely abundant. When you receive from Source, God expands and the Great Universe fills with even more love. This is the "as above" that we will teach you how to bring to the "so below" of your financial debts, which are illusionary from the perspective of Heaven.

Dissolving Financial Debt with Understanding and Love

We wish to teach you what each of your debts is helping you to learn about yourself. Understanding the subconscious and symbolic messages of each debt will make it easier for you to forgive the self-doubt that is manifesting as financial debt. Forgiveness within yourself will turn into paying off the debts and having indebtedness erased from your daily life. Our debt erasure may take time; however, with patience and learning, you will find that you not only become debt free, but you also find gratitude for the debts. Gratitude for your experiences will reinstate your innocence and have you trusting in your true, authentic, wealthy self.

Financial indebtedness is not your fault; however, it can be your joy to dissolve it with love once you comprehend what the miraculous insight debt can provide. You may also find that paying your taxes, household bills, and mortgage become happy events instead of something to dread and put off to the last minute. On Schoolroom Earth, everything is symbolic, and when the ego surrenders to the knowing that you are the creator of your reality, life can only get better. Yes, we are saying that you—ego, subconscious, and Soul—create the financial debts to mirror back to you the doubt and fear that are hiding within. You are not to blame yourself or anyone else for your financial debts because shame, blame, and guilt will only make the debts more resistant to transformation. Those who never experience having financial debt will need to learn the lesson of doubt in a different way and in a way that may be far more difficult.

Debt is the outer manifestation of your believing (please notice the word *lie* in the word *believing*) that you are less than because someone else has more money than you do. Have you ever felt less than because you compared yourself to another, or they compared themselves to you? Comparison is a trick of the old male and old female. They are ingenious at having you compare yourself to others and making the deduction that you are less than them.

Let's look at a list of areas where you may feel less than someone else. As you read each of the following, take note of where you feel shortchanged by Creator.

- Money and access to money, including inheritances, financial support, and gifts of money
- Beauty and physical attributes, including height, weight, strength, eye color, skin color, and age
- Intelligence, including the ability to be innovative, mathematical, musical, intuitive, clever, creative, highly skilled, and very knowledgeable (or well educated)
- Connections with influential people, including family with status and power in the world, access to resources and expertise of successful persons, and luck with being at the right place, at the right time, with the right people
- Charm, popularity, social graces, and social courage, including having admirable communication skills and negotiation poise
- Luck with money, including finding money, winning money, earning money, and multiplying money through investing

- Lovability and worthiness to be supported by Mother-Father-God, Divine Oneness, including feeling loved, wanted, and accepted by your parents, family, friends, community, and society

Please read our list a few times to see if you contract in your body or find that you are holding your breath. This is your body's way to confirm what your subconscious is recognizing as true.

We ask that as you read through the following healing experience, pay attention to your body and to your breathing. Your entire being always wants to let go of lies and fear. Undiluted love and Trust work like a plunger on the misconceptions that human beings can have about themselves. Let the lies go and invite the healing love and liberation to flow!

Healing Experience
Conquering Doubt

Close your eyes and breathe deeply. Step through the purple door and see before you a winding staircase that leads up to your library of beliefs. Walk up the stairs and find your divine inner child sitting on the counter, talking with the guardian Angel librarian.

Your first assignment is to ask the guardian Angel to turn on the large violet-fire sprinklers and shower the library entrance. The old male and old female are hiding behind the potted plants located behind the librarian's desk. If you don't clear them, they will find a way to distract you from entering the main room of your library.

When you enter the main room of the library, you will notice to your right, a towering vortex of sapphire blue and to your left, a vortex of aqua and gold. Greet Archangel Michael (sapphire blue) and Archangel Gabriel (aqua and gold) and say, "Thank you for helping me clear the doubts, lies, and insecurities that I have about myself."

Inside the main room we have placed a violet-fire dumpster lined with sapphire blue coals. There are Angels on tall ladders everywhere, tossing books (which contain lies) into the dumpster. Thank them for helping you.

Your divine inner child and Archangels Michael and Gabriel take you down the cellar stairs into the forgotten archives of your childhood and past lives. Say, "Wherever my limiting beliefs and doubts about myself and my connection to Source are, I release you. I forgive you and I return you to the Central Sun of Divine Oneness."

The floor beneath your feet turns violet, then emerald, and then ruby. There is a mass exodus of books that seem to be coming up out of the earth as well as from the shelves of the cellar walls. Feel this in your body and say, "Doubt out, love in. Doubt out, Trust in. Doubt out, faith in. Doubt out, love for Self IN!"

The Archangels return you to the main room of the library, and you notice that many books have vanished. Say, "Activate my self-worth and value as a divine child of Mother-Father-God/Creator/Divine Oneness, NOW." Watch as golden light-emanating books with new truths about you begin to fill the once empty shelves. A rainbow geyser of undiluted love now stands where the violet-fire dumpster was before. The energy is filling your library with Truth.

Your divine inner child opens an invisible door to your right, and you can see your creativity garden through the opening of the library's wall. The divine inner child points to a large chest at your feet that blocks the doorway. When you open the chest, you find a giant book with the title, *Your Creative Efforts Are Never Enough to Pay Off Debt or Generate Financial and Personal Freedom for You.*

Ask Archangel Michael of the Central Sun to pierce the giant book with his sapphire blue-flame Sword of Truth, Justice, and Victory. Watch the book turn to white dust.

Archangel Gabriel takes out her trumpet and soon the white dust has formed into a bird flying straight to the Central Sun.

Step into your creativity garden with the Angels. Thank your garden for growing projects, new ways of receiving abundance, and opportunities to share the fruits of your harvests now and in the future.

Rejoice in the beautiful chorus of the 12 Archangels singing that you are loved, wanted, treasured, supported, and well provided for all your days. Let there be no doubt remaining of who you truly are, Child of God!

Trust, together with gratitude, is the high-vibe magic elixir in which to dissolve financial debt. Below, we will explain a few of the most common debts to help your ego to see that having debt in your life is providing you with an opportunity to learn, not to feel punished.

THE SYMBOLIC MEANING OF COMMON FINANCIAL DEBTS

Taxes

Taxes are symbolic of responsibility, especially for one's parents and family. When back taxes are owed, or there are not enough funds to pay the taxes due, leap into the violet-fire river. Release the selves within that had to grow up before their time and felt that there was not enough of what they needed. If this does not resonate with you, try releasing the selves within you that feel that they have been abandoned by the Great Universe and feel like overwhelmed and helpless children. Stay in the violet-fire river until the color changes to ruby. Soak in the ruby love of the Divine Mother of the Great Universe and say, "Thank you Divine Mother for manifesting all the funds I need to pay off the taxes. I allow and I am thankful!"

Mortgages and Home Loans

A mortgage is symbolic of parental security, especially that of the mother. When you take out a mortgage either from a bank or from a private lender, you are symbolically receiving emotional and physical support from surrogate parents. Understand that nothing is permanent in your life, not even the home that you buy, because eventually you will return to Heaven. While on the Earth, your physical home is symbolic of your body, and your biological parents gave the cells for your beginning. Your mother provided you with your very first home, her womb. When you need a mortgage, your Soul is giving you the message, through your life experience, that you need to consistently fill up with Divine Mother and Divine Father of the Great Universe's love, positive attention, affection, and acknowledgment that you are valued, safe, secure, and free. To pay off your mortgage or home loan, acknowledge your true parents, the divine feminine and divine masculine aspects of Soul. Say, "Thank you, my divine feminine and my divine masculine, for providing for me in all ways." It may sound too simple; however, when the ego accepts that Soul has full responsibility of your being, then you will no longer need the experience of a bank owning your physical residence. Be patient as your mind may take time to release beliefs that tell you that there is no other way for you to own a home than to be in bondage to the "old male" bank or lender.

Auto Loan or Lease

An automobile is symbolic of how you are moving through life at the current time. If you are needing to finance your car then your Soul is trying to let you know that you are still carrying doubts about your belief that you deserve to be free to live the life you want to live, doing what you want to do, and going where you want to go. Please fill your automobile with turquoise, the energy of freedom and dreams come true, when you drive your car. It may be a more logical choice for you to lease your car; however, visualizing your car in turquoise singing light will benefit you in all ways moving forward.

Credit Card Debt

Credit cards are symbolic of giving yourself the credit and validation that your ego needs and deserves. Often this credit includes attention and acknowledgment of being your wonderful self, so you use the cards to purchase items that you may not have the immediate cash to purchase but nevertheless feel you deserve.

When you cannot pay off the full balance, you might be feeling unworthy of receiving because you do not feel valuable. Revolving credit card debt is a message that your ego feels unworthy and not good enough, no matter how convincing the external circumstances may seem to rationalize the debt. To open new revenue sources so that your Soul can pay off the debts through your financial reality, fill up with unconditional acceptance, gratitude, and approval of yourself daily. Also, we highly recommend that you repeat the exercise "Releasing the Puppet Strings of Attachment to Money" on page 114. You can be certain that fear's old male and old female like having you drowning in credit card debt. They want your ego to doubt your Soul's ability to rescue you.

Credit cards may also be a substitute for the magic parent that always says, "Yes, you can have what you want." When you find yourself buying things that you don't really want or need, please be compassionate with the hurting child or self within. You are crying out for a parent who loves you. This parent is your Soul. As you allow Divine Oneness and Soul to fill you with the love you have been missing, greater income will flow in. You will also be more discerning about what you wish to purchase for yourself. We are not saying that you will spend less, we are saying that you won't need to feel guilty and ashamed for giving yourself what you want. This will be mirrored in paying off your credit cards in full and no longer carrying a revolving balance.

Healing Experience
Credit and Validation for You

Close your eyes and step through the purple door. As your feet touch the emerald ground, allow Heart energy to fill you from below while the Central Sun fills you from above. Walk to the ruby pool where your divine inner child, divine feminine, and divine masculine wait for you.

As you step into the ruby pool of the Divine Mother's healing love, allow yourself to feel like a dehydrated, worn out "bag of bones." Your divine feminine offers you a cup of ruby tea that tastes very refreshing. Say, "I welcome my vessel to be saturated with acceptance of myself, unconditional love for myself, unconditional approval of myself, validation of my intelligence and ability, and gratitude for the fruits of my creativity garden."

The pool turns violet. Release any guilt, shame, blame, victim consciousness, unfairness, resentment, and anger. Breathe it all out and say, "I forgive myself. I forgive my life. I forgive everyone in my life that I feel has been unfair to me. I release my desire for a magic parent to rescue me, and I surrender to the care and overflowing generosity of Soul."

A rainbow waterfall appears and soaks your every cell, especially your hurting ego, with undiluted love and prosperity. Ask your divine inner child, "What can I do to increase my receiving from Source?" Listen, relax, and let the Trust soak in.

SHORT-TERM PERSONAL LOANS

A personal loan from a friend, family member, work associate, or finance company is a message that you are losing energy to a crisis in the past. This reacting in the present because of an experience in the past may have become a repetitive pattern. What is happening is that the hamster-in-the-wheel self feels like it needs to survive no matter how much it is running on empty. A short-term loan is like grabbing a high-sugar snack or a caffeine beverage so that you can keep going even though you are exhausted. The amount of the loan is irrelevant, although it can be a sign of your level of exhaustion. Needing to borrow a small amount of cash to tide you over may indicate that you could use a couple of days of mental rest in nature, while borrowing a large sum of money may indicate that you are burned out from your load of responsibilities. It can be helpful to look at the wealth you are allowing yourself to receive today. Thank the Divine Mother for receiving in more than what you need. Thank your Soul and Angels for creating the space for you to take a rest, especially if you do not see how this is possible. Say, "I am willing to experience the miracle of creating the time for rest and reflection." While you are resting, please repeat the healing experience "Credit and Validation for You" on page 122. If you are too tired to focus your mind, simply ask your divine inner child, divine feminine, and divine masculine to do it for you.

Our last recommendation for dissolving debt and self-doubt using the Power of undiluted love is to ask yourself the question, "Does financial hardship seem to run in my family?" Have you noticed your siblings, parents, aunts, uncles, cousins, or grandparents struggling to bring in the money they need? Do any family members barely keep their heads above water financially? Are they suffering from chronic financial stress? Are you willing to help yourself and your family dissolve the old story of not enough? In families where there is a history of addiction, even if money is not the issue, there can be underlying anxiety about not feeling valuable and worthy. These fears can be passed to the next generation and show up as doubt turned to debt. We offer you a simple yet powerful solution to put family indebtedness to rest.

Healing Experience
Transforming Family Patterns of Debt

Close your eyes. Breathe in deeply and slowly. Say, "I forgive the doubt and debt for all of us."

Step through the purple door and step into the violet-fire ocean of transformation and forgiveness.

Your divine inner child is with you and has a sack carrying the alphabetical letters in your family name. Help your divine inner child empty the sack of letters into the violet-fire ocean and say, "I forgive the debt for all of us. I forgive any shame, blame, poverty, or lack consciousness held in the letters of our name. I choose love for all of us, and I choose for all of us to be filled with undiluted love and Trust from Source."

If you feel that the story of financial debt or self-doubt is your own personal story and not shared with other family members, then ask your divine inner child to give you the sack with the letters in your first name (and middle name if you have one) and place these letters in the violet-fire ocean. For example, if your first name is Jill then the letters J, I, L, and L are in the sack. Say, "I release my old story of doubt. I lack nothing because I Am a Child of God. I forgive it all, even if it feels unforgivable. I matter to Divine Oneness. I am significant, and what I create and have to share is very valuable. I invite my Angels to help me know my worth and to teach me how to live debt free and doubt free. This I allow!"

Transform into a dolphin and swim out into the deep ocean until you come to a white fire vortex. From this super love-charged place, say, "I release any chronic financial worry that lives within my molecules and atoms. I release any doubt about my ability to grow wonderful things in my creativity garden. I allow myself to be saturated with the ruby love of the Divine Mother, and I welcome her to receive miracles, opportunities, and wealth through me. I allow and I give thanks!" Transform back into yourself and relax in the healing violet and white-fire energy.

The entire ocean turns turquoise and gold. Soul restores your human vessel with all that you are, and you stand up and reach your hands to the Central Sun. Say, "I call my self-esteem back to me. I call my personal power back to me. I call my independence and success that is my birthright into my humanity, NOW!"

One more tool to help you stop worrying about money, keep your vibration up, and hold on to your energy is to ask your guardian Angels to make you aware of your money thoughts. When your thoughts are not focused on thanking the Great Universe for the prosperity flowing to you, then put all things concerning money in the violet-fire ocean. This might be your wallet, bank statements, tax returns, financial investment portfolio, and credit score. Ship all money-related thoughts out to the violet-fire sea for transformation of the fear held within. If you are still unable to shift your money thoughts out of anxiety and into trust, then repeat the healing exercise, "Releasing the Puppet Strings of Attachment to Money," on page 114. Once you have done the clearing, thank the money that you have received for multiplying for you and for the sender. Remember, money is a thoughtform that has been saturated with fear. For money to come to you, help the money thoughtform rise in vibration by using gratitude and trust in Source. To help the Central Sun provide financial relief, we need to connect the thoughtform of money to creativity. Creativity forces the fear out of money and takes it out of the controlling hands of the old male and old female and gives it to you. Let us teach you how this works!

Are you ready to receive more from the Great Universe by allowing your creativity garden to change your financial reality? We need to help you clear some seductive fear-based beliefs that may sound rational. These beliefs tell you that being creative is not enough to change your current or future financial reality. Any fear-based belief is made of illusion and has no power when you use Heart Power to attract your success. Success and creative expression go together. It's time to transform the most convincing old male and old female beliefs that limit your receiving of prosperity from your creative output.

Creativity and Sustainable Flow

Making yourself do what you do not want to do will only cause you to feel sad and angry. Frustration creates drought for your garden. Along with a creativity drought, when your ego mind connects the value of your harvest to what it expects others are willing to pay, trouble ensues. We need to challenge the ego's calculations and tell you that harvesting a pound of potatoes does not equal the going market price for potatoes. Your creative expression and contribution are invaluable. They are priceless. Every original creation and Heart-centered service you offer to another is priceless in the eyes of Creator. Respect what grows in your creativity garden!

We need the ego to detach from what you have been told you will earn from the wealth that Mother-Father-God wants you to have and will send to you. When you put a price tag on your worth, you limit the flow of what you are open to receive from the Great Universe. We understand that you need to price the fruits of your harvest to sell them. This is different, vibrationally, from associating the real value of your creative efforts with any amount of money. Ask your Helpers in Heaven to give the best monetary price for the fruit. They will repeat the number, through your intuition, until it is crystal clear in your mind. Also, it is one thing to offer a sample of fruit from your garden, but it is quite another to give your entire harvest away as that will only attract those who expect free fruit. This does not help them or you to receive from Source.

The ego, when confused by the trickery of fear's old male and female, may believe that the best income can only come from work that appears to have the greatest earning potential. When financial success does not look like the ego expects, then you may doubt your own value. This is exactly what the old male and old female hope you will do. However, if you focus on being happy and excited about developing your creative ideas, your pipeline to Source stays open and resources flow to you.

Let's transform the beliefs that limit the income you allow yourself to receive from both expected and unexpected income streams. Moving these pipeline blockers out of the way will help you to experience a new financial reality. Trust that your Soul is providing for you, through your own creative efforts, as well as in surprisingly miraculous ways. Creativity keeps the pipeline open between you and the Divine Mother of the Great Universe. The Divine Mother receives abundance for you as energy. The energy of love then manifests as what you need in daily life. This is the wisest way to receive sustainable financial resources that you can trust belong to you. We cannot repeat this often enough: keeping your creative expression clear means that you do what makes you and your divine inner child feel happy. Raising the vibration of your ego mind to that of your divine masculine keeps you courageous and helps you share your joy-filled harvest. Unblocking creativity keeps the pipeline open for you to receive in a reliable, sustainable, and trustworthy financial flow.

Please look at the list of creativity- and money-pipeline blockers below. As you read each one, see if you hold your breath or feel anxiety in your body. Although some of the blockers may sound perfectly logical, they do not help your creativity to flow. Abundant and joyful creativity is necessary to tap into Source's direct flow. We can help get things flowing once you identify the blocks that need to be released and sent to the Central Sun.

► Financial- and Creative-Flow
Pipeline Blockers

- Money comes to me through hard work and constant effort.
- I have experienced that there is no one out there who can really help me, so it is better if I "grin and bear it."
- There is just too much pressure on me to think about being creative or consider the possibility that life could be different.
- Either I have worked for the money, or I will work for it. I'm the one who does the work and provides the money.
- Creativity only gets in the way of earning reliable money.
- You must do the work that pays you. Forget about loving what you do.
- Take any job that you can get if it will pay you well.
- Risk-taking usually leads to failure. Best to play it safe.
- If I don't earn the money, it's not my money.
- The only person that I can count on is myself.
- I don't value or respect the results of my creative efforts.
- Be cautious of those who say they want to help you. What do they expect for their assistance?
- Stick to the tried-and-proven jobs if you want to survive on Earth.
- Earning a paycheck from an employer is far better than working for myself.
- I identify as being the female and therefore must be provided for by a male (or old male job).
- I identify as being the male, and I am expected to be the provider (even if I hate my job).
- I identify as the female who is expected to care and provide for everyone.
- I'm not creative.
- Money doesn't come easily to me.

- Earning and having lots of money is more important than happiness (and doing the work that makes me feel like I'm not working).
- I don't have the startup funds to begin a creative project.
- I need to have the money before I can start a creative project.
- The only way I can see having the money I need to live the way I want is to win the lottery or have my financial investments go through the roof.
- Not enough people want what I have to offer.
- Angels can't help me with money because they don't need money where they live.
- I don't have the time or energy to be creative.
- I can't possibly support myself financially through sharing the harvest of my creativity garden. I don't have what it takes to do this.
- I don't trust that the Divine Mother of the Great Universe can receive money into my earthly reality.
- I don't trust that the Divine Father of the Great Universe can provide clear directions on what I can do to earn money in a way that makes me happy.
- I don't trust that Soul can provide for my financial needs through my creative expression.
- I don't trust that my divine inner child can use Heart Power to draw to me the help that I need to support myself financially.
- I don't trust that I can be of service to the greater good and focus on earning a living at the same time.
- I don't trust that I can manage my emotional sensitivity and function in a money-driven world.

Feel free to add to our list if you have discovered some other convincing and limiting beliefs running through your brain.

Healing Experience
Clearing the Pipeline

Ask your divine inner child to show you if the pipeline blocker is the size of a small stone or the size of a mountain. If you are not a visualizer then trust what you feel. If you are not sure, then go with mountain size.

Ask your guardian Angels, Helpers in Heaven, and divine masculine and divine feminine to push the mountain (or stone) into the violet-fire ocean. See the mountain disappear under the violet-fire water and say, "I release this blocker for good. Out you go, old male and old female limiting belief! I forgive myself for believing the lie!"

Return to the list and put the next blocker into the violet-fire ocean. Repeat, "I release this blocker for good. Out you go, old male and old female limiting belief!" If it's easier, put the entire list in the violet-fire ocean and say, "I release any and all creative and financial blockers from my vessel, and I forgive them all."

Once the stones and mountains have dissolved, the violet ocean will change into emerald, bright green, and gold. Step into the green ocean with your divine inner child and team of Helpers in Heaven. Say, "Thank you for saturating my ego with Trust and respect for my divinity. Thank you for pouring Trust into the deep subconscious where I store my lack of trust. I am willing to open my pipeline!"

For the joy of it, return to your creativity garden and look to see what genius ideas your Soul has planted for you to change your financial reality. And if you do not discover anything remarkable, hold on. We are going to introduce the "community garden" soon. For now, we ask you to breathe, surrender, and let trust and respect fill you.

Now that you are willing to use the harvest from your garden to increase your financial flow, here is a tool to assess what you need to change to move from financial stress to sustainable wealth. Remember, we define wealth as happiness. As a divine child of Mother-Father-God, you are completely deserving of doing the work that pays you more than you need and has you feeling full of joy and purpose.

❀

Healing Experience
Receive, Attract, Focus, and Grow!

Please ask yourself if you need help with receiving. Do you need more money, clients, opportunities, or customers? Are you afraid that you won't have enough money for the short-term or long-term future? Do you feel that your creativity or your financial flow is stuck, and you need things to move forward? Could you use more support in your daily life? If your answer is yes, jump into the violet-fire river and say, "Old male, OUT! Divine feminine and Divine Mother, IN!"

Stay in the violet river until the color changes to ruby. Soak in the ruby undiluted love until you feel fully saturated with safety, security, and unconditional love.

Ask yourself if you need help with focusing on what to do? Do you need clear direction? Do you want to identify what is next to harvest from your creativity garden? Do you want to know what to charge for a product or service? Do you need the courage to take a leap of faith? Do you need to know what to do to earn money, spend money, or share money? If your answer is yes, jump into the violet-fire river and say, "Old female, OUT! Divine masculine and Divine Father, IN!"

Stay in the violet river until the color changes to turquoise and sapphire blue. See yourself as a tall, empty glass and fill up with the colors of clear focus, courage, truth, and strength.

Ask yourself if life has become all work and no play. Do you have difficulty in trusting yourself or trusting others? Do you have trouble asking for help or asking for what you want from a loved one or a stranger? Are you afraid of being hurt because of your sensitivity? Are you having trouble attracting the qualified and reliable support needed to care for the fruit trees in your garden? Are you finding it challenging to trust that customers will come? If your answer is yes, jump into the violet-fire river and say, "I send my wounded children and all wounded selves to the Central Sun for healing. I do this with love and compassion. I welcome in the trust of my divine inner child and the glorious liberation of the Central Sun.

Stay in the violet fire until the river becomes all the colors of Creator's rainbow. Say, "Divine inner child, divine feminine, and divine masculine of Soul, lead me to a happy childhood NOW!"

Ask yourself if you are allowing your work to evolve. Do you love what you do for a living? If you do not need to earn money, do you love what is happening in your creativity garden? Are you fulfilling the calling of your Soul and making a positive difference in the lives of others? Do you feel that you are living in more of Heaven's vibration every day? If your answer is no to any of our questions, then jump into the white-fire vortex that we have made for you. Say, "I call on the aid of the 12 Archangels of the Central Sun to help me surrender to the great and vast wealth that I Am."

Stay in the white-fire vortex until it changes to opalescent. Step out of the vortex and enter the community garden.

THE COMMUNITY GARDEN

As we work together to help you express the genius pouring into your brain from the Central Sun, you may find that you desire to work with others who are also Heart centered. The community garden is a place where your creative ideas merge, flow, and collaborate with the abilities and passions of others. For example, let's say that you and your divine inner child love to make desserts and when you step into the community garden, you attract to you a chef who enjoys creating the main course. The chef knows the perfect farmer who can provide the eggs and butter for your cakes. The farmer knows the finest event planner in all the land. All the divine inner children within each of you enjoy using your Heart Power to attract customers to your shared table. When Souls gather and egos surrender, the highest vibrational magic happens, and abundance multiplies. Respect for your own creative pursuits as well as respect for all helps the orchard grow and the produce to multiply. Drought can attack the garden if old male's control or old female's "poor me" enter the scene. It is recommended that each person does what they do best and leave the tending of their neighbor's garden to their neighbor. Evolution will happen in the community garden. Change will come. Some gardeners will leave, and new gardeners will join the community. If you allow your Helpers in Heaven to help with the management and stay connected to your feelings and the twin sisters, all will go surprisingly well.

Community gardens do not work well when there is an old male and old female hierarchy. We recommend that when there are profits to be shared that they are shared equitably and generously. The Great Universe is always giving. Where there is kindness, respect, and true community, Source will make sure that the harvest is greater than expected. And if a community project turns to dust and does not produce even a piece of fruit for one of you, don't give up. Look at what needs to be changed and celebrate all that you have learned. This is a schoolroom after all, and each gardener is learning to value love over fear. When team efforts don't deliver, be patient and trust that something better has already taken root in the garden.

We invite you to move your life out of the sensibility of lack and into abundance. Once your financial reality has transformed, do some inner reflection and ask Soul if anything else could be improved in your life. You, divine Child of the Central Sun, are worthy of having all your emotional and physical needs met. If the need is an ego need and not something that you truly want with your Heart and Soul, then it can be helpful to become aware of this. Our intention is to encourage you to feel what your humanity needs to be happy and to receive it from Source, especially when you don't believe this is possible.

PART 5

What Is Still Missing?

The Law of As Above, So Below tells you that you can live in Heaven on Earth. Why would you accept less than Heaven's jubilee?

THE 12 ARCHANGELS OF THE CENTRAL SUN

The 12 Archangels' Formula to Change Your Reality

As frustrating as Schoolroom Earth may appear when you view life from your human perspective, we have good news to share. All attending Schoolroom Earth are evolving in consciousness. Evolution is happening even with the intensity of the dramas playing out on the global screen. We ask that you step back and imagine that every human being is the star of their own movie, and their movie is playing in their own theater. If you focus on what you are experiencing in your movie and use your spiritual tools to edit it, then you help all other movies shift in vibration. This is not selfish or heartless. You are actually a positive reality changer, a present-day shamanic force working for the good of all.

Bring your awareness back home to yourself and ask, "What is missing from my life that would bring me greater happiness?" What the ego may not know is that Soul has already been whispering your desires to you through your divine inner child. When you are consciously aware of what is missing from your current reality, the miracle of changing your movie has begun! Angels encourage you to fill your life with the wealth of Heaven because as your happiness increases, you become an accelerator of evolution for all. Below, we offer you our six-step formula, working with the singing colors of the Central Sun, to help you receive what Soul desires for you to experience.

1. Ask yourself, "What is missing from the movie of my life that would bring me fulfillment while still supporting my evolution into a wiser and kinder person?" Say, "Thank you, Divine Mother of the Great Universe, together with the divine inner child of my Soul, for receiving what is missing into my life. Thank you, Angels, for helping me to stay out of my own way of receiving this blessing!" Visualize yourself, or hold the intention, of being saturated in ruby singing light.

2. Check to see if any hurts and fears in your subconscious are driving what your ego thinks is missing from your movie. The ego, influenced by the past, can put such strong limits on what he wants the picture of happiness to look like that it can create incredible anxiety and displeasure. Let go of the timing, and the "how" of what is missing will come to you. Check our list of subconscious motivations and be sure to fill your subconscious with the healing energy needed. Say, "I release the past. I forgive the past. I no longer want to live in a past that limits my present and future." Ask your guardian Angels to shower you with violet fire. And let it go.

3. Ask yourself, "What picture, person, timing, or way my dream will come true am I attached to experiencing?" When you are aware that the ego is attached to a certain outcome, give the picture, as well as any anxiety it creates, to Soul. Hand it all to Mother-Father-God. Visualize yourself, or hold the intention of, standing in a vortex of sapphire singing light.

4. Give thanks to Creator that what was lacking has now been replaced with Heaven's abundance. Try to feel what it is like to have your desire fulfilled by your Soul and the Great Universe. For example, if you want friendship, what does a real, loyal, and trustworthy friend feel like? Ask your Soul and Angels to flood you with the feeling of happiness and gratitude for your own value, as well as the vibration of a loving community. The divine laws will be activated immediately to support receiving. What is within you will manifest

in your daily life when you do your part by keeping fear's old male and female from lowering your vibration. Give thanks if what you receive is not what the ego expects and know it means that you have something even better coming. Visualize, or hold the intention of, dancing together with your divine inner child in the rainbow colors of gratitude. Let the singing rays of the Central Sun move through you and replenish any place within that needs more love, trust, and respect.

5. Let go of trying to change another person's movie or redecorate their theater to match your own. Express your compassion by transforming your own life and then work with the powerful colors of undiluted love to fill the theaters of those in despair. Love is the greatest Power and instead of lowering your own vibration to that of sympathy, pity, disgust, anger, and indignation, send love where love is missing. This act of generosity helps you to receive and those you wish to help to shift in consciousness so that they, too, can receive. Visualize, or hold the intention of, putting yourself and the person you have concerns about in the violet-fire river. Focus on the violet until it changes to ruby, Divine Mother's love. Soak in the ruby love until you are completely saturated and then do the same for the one you wish to help.

6. Ask your divine inner child to plug into the Heart Power of the Central Sun and fill you with Trust and respect for your divinity. Keep asking to be filled with confidence in your Soul and faith in Source. Fill up with trust that your team of Helpers in Heaven can help you to open and receive what you want or something even better than what the ego can fathom. Visualize, or hold the intention, that you are a tree with deep roots being nurtured by a vortex of emerald and other shades of vibrant green. See your branches and leaves being lit and brightened by the Central Sun. Let the colors mix and say, "I am the miracle of Trust in every atom of my being, the divine united with the human."

Because your subconscious can contribute up to 90 percent of the movie you are living, taking responsibility for what is missing in your life and asking your Soul to give it to you is essential. It is also essential to transform the fear of the past and experience positive and lasting change today. To move from lack to abundance, we ask that you do the following in an incarnation: Love another unconditionally and receive unconditional love, experience freedom from fear in your mind and choices, respect your physical body for the divinity and wisdom it offers you, and choose to know and live the true purpose of Soul.

To graduate from Schoolroom Earth, you will need to transform most of the theoretical 90 percent of fear stored in the subconscious caverns. Transformation of fear is why you have chakras and why the Central Sun has rays that penetrate your atoms. Your chakra energies lift you and hold you in the Heart of God.

We invite you to count on our support, every moment of every incarnation. Would you like this life to reach the elusive state of divine grace (peacefulness and trust) while on Earth? When you can redirect the lower vibrational energy that erupts from remembering past events, freedom is yours to enjoy. Letting go of the past whenever you recognize that you are still reacting from an old, wounded place opens you to receive abundance and complete liberation. Divine human beings, you can do this before returning to Heaven. Grace may only last for a few moments, but it will grow inside of you. As you let us guide you in connecting deeper with the all-loving Source of your Soul, you will understand the value of undiluted love.

To Love and
Be Loved

To help you feel what unconditional, divine love feels like, we recommend you walk in nature and hug a tree. Once you can feel the vast undiluted love that the tree sends to you and emits out into the environment, you might consider adopting or purchasing a dog or cat, or both. Pets go through special Angel training before they come to Schoolroom Earth to be equipped with the wisdom and behavior that will help you grow. They may even choose to take on hardship to end up with the family that they know belongs to them. Pets are on a mission: to teach humans how to laugh and how to love, even when this means that they may be abused during your training. They understand that they will push your buttons and reflect the emotional neediness of your inner child by being purposefully demanding of your time and attention. A pet trained in the heavenly realms will know what to break, chew, pee on, and destroy to teach patience, forgiveness, and understanding and how to get in touch with your buried emotion. Like the trees, they will flood your being with unconditional, undiluted love at every opportunity.

When a dog gives you her belly to rub, or a cat graces you with a purr while you pet him, your empty emotional buckets are being filled to overflowing. Before you consider asking Soul to bring you a loving relationship with someone, who may not have an ego evolved enough to reciprocate your affections, learn to value hugging a tree, rubbing a dog belly, and scratching a cat under the chin for the great joy this will give you.

When you seek a real love relationship, whether this is a romantic one or a true friendship, think about the qualities that you desire this person to have and ask Soul to give you these qualities. Soul will ask the ego to look at why you feel you need a real love relationship for your life on Schoolroom Earth to be complete. If your answer is to help you to grow emotionally and spiritually because you know that this person will mirror aspects about yourself that you cannot see, then you are on the fast track to bringing in love. Seeking companionship is natural and organic for human beings. Soul will ask that you be your own best friend and until you live this, relationships with family, friends, and lovers may leave you wanting. Forgiveness of the past is imperative to opening your life to receiving love from another. Even if you believe you have forgiven the abuse and disappointment from past lovers, keep forgiving them until you are free of any pain that the memories invoke.

If your life is missing a long-term romantic partner, someone to share a home and life with, then be sure to ask your wounded child if they are seeking a magic parent to provide something that you would prefer not to provide for yourself. Long-term partnership comes with plenty of compromise and entails learning to love and respect yourself unconditionally and doing the same for your partner. A real relationship requires that you learn to stop assuming the other person knows what's on your mind. Relationship is essential in learning how to communicate with honesty and truth with yourself and greatly supports the evolution of the ego.

Relationship also encourages the ego to let go of control and surrender to Soul's direction. Long-term partnership is an important lesson that will be repeated until you learn to respect your own needs and let go of hoping that someone else will fulfill them. When Soul feels that a romantic relationship will be a distraction to your taking care of your own emotional and physical needs, then Soul will prevent you from finding the right match until you fall in love, completely, with your own divine inner child.

Look at the relationships that you have had in the past. Do any of these people remind you of your mother, father, or other disappointing or missing care provider in your childhood? If you are disappointed in your friendships, then look at what you wish your friends would give to you and give this list to yourself. Soon you will have friends entering your theater and playing important and positive roles in your movie without expecting more from them than what they can give. Forgiving your missing or rejecting parent or anyone else in the past who hurt your feelings will stop you from attracting abandoning and rejecting lovers. Seeing all who hurt you standing under the violet-fire waterfall works great for transforming the past! Forgiving the past helps your Heart open to real love.

How will you know when your Soul is giving the "green light" for a real love relationship? Soul will fill the ego with calmness, patience, and Trust. This state of mental grace helps you to hear Soul's directions for what to do, if anything, to help your beloved find you. For some, the internet can work well, and for others, asking Soul to set the stage so that you bump into your Heart's mate works perfectly. Soul, together with your team of matchmaking Angels, will make sure that you and your perfect match find one another. What can feel wonderful for your ego is to write a letter to God and list what matters most to your Heart. What values do you wish your partner to have in common with you? It may feel like a big relief to list qualities that your last lover did not have and that you now understand are deal breakers for you, such as honesty, availability, integrity, and the willingness to transform and grow with you.

Moving on from the past is crucial to bringing in a real love relationship and if you do not have such a relationship in your reality then continue to forgive the past no matter how victimized you may still feel.

Releasing the negative emotions, resentments, and fear that you might be abused again makes room within you for real love to find you. The Law of As Above, So Below, As Within, So Without will call your partner to you in the way that works for your own greatest good and highest joy and the greatest good and highest joy for your partner. Relationships help you to learn how to acknowledge your boundaries and communicate them to others. All relationships are valuable; even the ones where you get hurt. Transform the hurt with loving-kindness and forgiveness, learn more about what you need in a relationship, and invite in a much happier love story. And remember: guardian Angels are gifted therapists.

Thank the divine inner child for bringing in new relationships that mirror where you are presently on your journey. Allow your friendships and relationships to evolve and if there is a toxic family member, know that taking care of yourself may very well be what you need to learn how to do. You can still love them and have compassion for them, even if it is best to do this from a safe distance. To keep yourself in an abusive or punishing situation is never what Soul will ask you to endure once you have learned that your happiness and well-being are priceless. It may be something that you experienced in childhood as the foundation for the lessons needed to be learned in this life, but it is not something to be endured once you recognize that you are suffering or sacrificing yourself to make someone else happy.

Real love relationships are essential to living a wealthy life and worth your highest vibrational intentions to experience them. We remind you that spending time in your creativity garden helps you to receive. If you are waiting for a special someone to come into your life, give your desire to your divine inner child to go find the very best playmate for you and then go and do something creative. The Divine Mother, together with your divine feminine, receives the lover into your reality. You are most receptive for love coming from others when you soak in ruby singing light. Ruby love saturates you with emotional security, physical safety, and unconditional love, approval, and acceptance.

Do this releasing and forgiving part of our healing experience for family members, friends, coworkers, and lovers before moving on to sending your invitation into the Great Universe.

Healing Experience
Forgiving the Past

Open your ribcage like it is a swinging door. Say, "I release my grief, sorrow, and heartache from relationships past but not forgotten." See dark hearts, shattered glass, and broken shells leave your heart area. Breathe in deeply, exhale slowly, and say, "I forgive it all, especially that which feels both unforgettable and unforgiveable. I forgive myself and I forgive them."

See and hear dark storm clouds with bits of lightning and thunder leave your heart area. Say, "I release all of my disappointments that they could not change. I release all my anguish in thinking their inability to change must be my fault. I forgive them their inability to love me in the way I needed love expressed. I forgive myself for not having what they wanted or needed to feel safe in a relationship with me, or I with them. I forgive myself for sacrificing my energy and time to please them so that they might reciprocate and value my love."

Walk through the purple door and into the violet-fire river of trans-formation and forgiveness. Once in the violet river, invite the energy to rise and say, "Out old male and old female thoughts telling me that I am not enough or that I did something wrong. Take your negative what-if-something-goes-wrong-again thoughts with you!"

Hold the hand of your divine inner child and the hand of your divine feminine. Say, "I release all of the guilt inside of me. I release any hurt feelings that tell me that I must be unlovable. I release all of my worry, fear, and anxiety that I will be alone all of my life."

Once the fear is out, the river will turn magenta and emerald with gold sparkles. Your divine masculine will join the three of you in the river. Say, "I invite my beloved partner (or new true friend) into my movie. Thank you, matchmaking Angels, for helping me to not sabotage myself. I allow real love to find me, teach me, and make me grow."

You are now ready to write your letter to the Divine Mother and Father. Tell them what you believe you are now ready to experience and surrender the past, present, and future to the Great Universe.

Are you experiencing freedom in your choices and daily responsibilities that you need and want to feel happy most of the time? We say "most of the time" because you may need to clear out fear's old male control and old female's guilt all of your days on Schoolroom Earth. If you believe that you do not have the freedom you want because you don't have enough money, we hope you find our next set of healing tools miraculous. A free mind is the most essential ingredient in the recipe for lasting happiness. Let's dive into what may be stealing your freedom because your subconscious believes it is the way life works. Reality changes from the inside out, and there may still be an ancient and harmful belief paradigm stuck in the root of your roots.

The Freedom to Choose

Religions may have good intentions; however, when mankind puts rules around the way a human needs to think and function, it interferes with the divine laws. The divine laws support your education to choose love and oneness over fear and separation. When patriarchal religious and government structure come together and freedoms are taken away, fear, judgment, and confusion impregnate the human collective. Under the guise of religion or righteous government, the old male and old female continue to influence humanity to keep the feminine hidden and allow the masculine to have the voice and power. Although the global movie is changing, the inner suppression of the feminine mind is mirrored in the outer reality where the human female and human child are evaluated as weaker and less than the human male.

We ask, "Why would the all-loving Creator of every Soul love some more than others or want some to have more freedom than others?" We are confident that as the human collective continues to evolve and wake up to the highest vibrational Truth, the confines of restrictive religions, governments, and dominating old-male egos will turn to dust. The Law of One tells you that every particle of the Great Universe belongs to the whole of Divine Oneness. As you regain the freedom to think for yourself and choose love and respect as being part of Divine Oneness, you help us to free all beings who are experiencing punishment and poverty.

It is part of our mission to help all who are willing to transform the deep subconscious history of slavery of the body and mind. Vanquishing the old male and old female out of religion so that love, honor, charity, and goodness remain will help you experience greater happiness and help all rise out of suffering. Like the secretive black box of money, the symbolic stone coffins of religion, cruel government policies, and old-male ego domination need to be returned to the Central Sun. The dense and formidable coffins store fear-laden belief paradigms that are entangled with deception and have the power to make you believe you are forbidden to go directly to God. One very old lie that needs to be released and transformed is that women and children are not allowed access to the riches of knowledge and abundance of the Great Universe. Old lies in the subconscious show up as lack of freedom, respect, and opportunity in your life today.

The outgrown beliefs that are driving your politicians, religious leaders, corporations, and governments are influencing your choices, from the subconscious level to the conscious level. Instead of recognizing the clear and higher vibrational choice of love, many human beings, even enlightened and aware human beings, are still feeling enslaved and find themselves suffering from exhaustion and the sacrifice of overworking. Do you feel disrespected and powerless in any aspect of daily life? Heavy feelings, responsibilities, and the frustrations that come with the responsibilities happen when you are unaware your mind is under the influence of hidden fears. Once these archaic beliefs are gone, the divine laws can fuel the freedom that has always been yours to experience. Please have compassion for your neighbor who may not be ready to let go and so they remain trapped in the old and familiar movie that once played in your own theater.

We will teach you how to release the death of your freedom (coffin) into the violet-fire sea for eternity and beyond. Like the puppet strings of money's black box, the stone coffin has shackles and handcuffs that keep you bound to the lie that fear protects you and keeps you safe. If you have experienced self-sacrifice, self-denial, unworthiness, poverty, or feelings of guilt, please look for another shackle—the heavy Christian cross. The traditional Christian symbol represents sacrifice and is cemented in the mind of the One Human Body. We awaken the Truth within your mind and Heart that the staff connecting Heaven to Earth, the original "cross," is far more ancient in origin than the one adopted by the Christian faith. The true staff of Truth is symbolic of your spine. We intend to flood your spine with love so that fear leaves your nervous system. Receive into your spinal cord the highest vibrational strength, Sound, and Light that will guide your life from the inside out.

Allow the symbol of the four-pointed cross, where the arms meet in the center, to return to its original representation—the five directions and five elements: the east representing the element of fire and the masculine, the south representing the mineral element and the inner child, the west representing the element of water and the feminine, the north representing the element of air and higher awareness, and the center of the cross representing the element of spirit and Divine Oneness. Raising the vibration of the Christian cross does not show disrespect to the true Christian values of love, kindness, and service for the greater good. Instead, it helps the subconscious of the One Human Body begin to break free from religious beliefs that intersect most of the religions that have existed or still exist. By visualizing the symbol of a cross (shaped like the human body, with the vertical piece being longer than the horizontal piece) dissolving in violet fire, you help the entire human collective choose love over fear. Holding the symbol of the cross in violet fire also works to clear slavery, punishment, abuse, thievery, and destruction of the human being. What does the cross of heavy burdens you carry need to say to you before you can forgive it? Are you ready to forgive the fear entrenched in aspects of the religion followed by members of your familial heritage? Love remains. Truth remains. We thank you for letting the fear return to God.

Our observation is that any religious and higher vibrational philosophy has value when it teaches a human being how to be honest, considerate, generous, compassionate, accepting, and respectful of self and others. When any office of any religion transforms into a truly loving spiritual community where every member has freedom of choice, all benefit.

Healing Experience

Transforming Fear Caused by Religion and Government

Take a deep sapphire blue breath of courage into your being and exhale helplessness. Repeat until you feel brave and strong.

See yourself walk around to your back. Gently pull at the handle that appears at the nape of your neck and then the handle that appears in your midback. Feel Archangel Michael of the Central Sun lift out this coffin through your hands and see it fly over your head and splash into the violet-fire ocean.

Say, "I release the lies of religion that hold me in guilt and punishment. I forgive it all. I choose love and freedom."

Step into the Divine Mother's ruby ocean and say, "I am thirsty!" Watch as the crosses that represent self-sacrifice and victimization by the dominating old-male ego leave your body. We send them to the Central Sun for you.

In the ruby ocean, see yourself looking at the front of your body. Gently pull the handle located on your forehead and the second handle on your heart. Feel Archangel Victoria of the Central Sun lift out the second coffin and see it fly over your head and splash into the violet-fire ocean.

Say, "I release the hidden lies, control, and deception in past and present institutional policies that hold me in the fear of change and the fear of the future. I forgive it all. I choose Heart Power and freedom!"

You are still standing in the Divine Mother's ruby ocean. Say again, "I am thirsty!" Watch as the shackles and chains (and there may be more crosses) fall away and dissolve in the ruby energy.

The ruby ocean changes to turquoise, the energy of freedom. Out through the top of your head, see the purging of the dominating old-male ego. Archangel Michael catches him and wraps him in purple duct tape and hands him off to Archangel Metatron. Metatron puts him in white fire, and he turns to dust. The Angels blow the dust to the Central Sun. All the old females attached to the dominating old-male ego come pouring out of the top of your head, and they are propelled to the Central Sun.

Say, "I release the indoctrination of the dominating old-male ego and I choose love to lead me forward to experience greater self-esteem and freedom on the hour. I open my mind and my being to receive positive change!"

A ray of the Central Sun becomes a swing of golden singing light. Your divine inner child is waiting for you on the swing. Archangel Metatron lifts you into the swing and gives you a good push.

Enjoy the flight and the refueling of your self-esteem and personal power by the Central Sun. After your solar plexus has been filled up, the swing gently comes to rest.

We transport you and your divine inner child to your creativity garden. What do you feel? What is growing for you? Creativity is freedom on Schoolroom Earth. Creativity is a flood of love pouring in from the Divine Mother of the Great Universe through your feminine mind. What do you love to do that gives you a sense of freedom and lasting joy?

Ask your divine inner child, "What is the true purpose of my Soul? What am I here on Earth to contribute for the greatest good and highest joy for all concerned?"

Living the Mission of Your Soul

Every Soul yearns for the ego to discover the real value and application of undiluted love in the multitude of mundane tasks required for daily life on Earth. The ego learning to accept the self without judgment, sarcasm, criticism, or comparison to another is a wonderful accomplishment for any Soul. And when the personality desires to express the vastness of their Soul's divinity, in all ways and in all things, Divine Oneness sings in jubilant chorus. We ask you to think of your personality as a train moving swiftly on a magnetic track, the force field of your Soul. Soul's responsibility is to keep you on track and if you derail off your purpose, Soul will wait patiently, persistently tugging the ego back into the highest vibrational flow of Source. Soul wants you to feel as happy as a delighted child, while also expressing your creative genius. Your Soul's mission can be as simple as encouraging smiles from others by smiling yourself and as intense as saving a life in an emergency operation.

The ego tends to measure self-worth by comparing his earthly accomplishments with those of others, while Soul asks, "Are you experiencing joy? Are your actions helpful to others? Have you done something kind for Mother Earth recently? Does your work fill you with love and gratitude?" And our favorite, "Are you having fun with your divine inner child?" If you are feeling traumatized, stressed out, and frustrated then please try to find a quiet place to breathe. Say, "I surrender to the joy of my Soul" and repeat this until you feel better. Soul wants you to stay on purpose and to do this, you need the ego to vibrate as close to the frequency of Soul as possible. Your Soul works continuously—especially during the most challenging lessons on Schoolroom Earth—to help you to feel good about who you are, the work you do, and the choices you make.

If Souls sent to Earth resonate at the vibration of loving-kindness, then how can some of their egos go so "off the rails?" Some Souls allow their egos to act as emotional triggers for the purpose of purging the subconscious for the human collective. When you are going through a challenging time in your own life, and you question if your Soul is helping you, then ask yourself if what you are experiencing is a subconscious purge. We call these events spiritual initiations. Once the challenging time is over, you will be clearer about who you are and better able to trust that your train is on the right track and in alignment with the divine laws.

Your Helpers in Heaven encourage you to practice letting go of questioning whether your train has been on the tracks or off the tracks for any part of life. Even when your train is derailed or parks itself for longer than you may like at the train depot, Soul is evolving through you. Your Soul will use every human experience to learn about love and will persistently be the "fly on the wall" of your consciousness to make sure that the ego integrates what Soul is mastering. And if this conversation between the ego and Soul does not go well during life on Earth, it will continue in life review once Soul and the personality return to Heaven. Living your Soul's purpose while you are visiting Schoolroom Earth helps all Divine Oneness evolve.

Soul is always living its mission through you and if the ego gets completely disconnected and trapped in fear, then Soul can create an exit out of Schoolroom Earth. Physical death cannot happen without permission from Soul, even in the case of suicide. What can you do to enjoy living your life to the fullest and partnering fully with your Soul so that you feel united in purpose? Communicate with the divine inner child that lives within you throughout the day. This simple practice will help the ego stay focused on what matters most to your Heart. This practice will help you to receive from the Great Universe and give you self-esteem, the fuel the ego needs to keep your emotions buoyed. Emotion is the real power that moves you forward so when you feel stuck in a rut, make sure you ask yourself, "What do I feel?" Feeling your feelings helps the ego feel positive and passionate about the purpose you are living!

Living your purpose is helped by taking the expectation to be perfect, along with the pressure to be everything to everyone, off your sensitive ego. Pressure is a magnet for the old male and old female to step right in, take over, and destroy. Given the opportunity, the old male pressures all egos to measure success by how much money and success they accumulate. He asks how fast they can accomplish what they want to get done or how much they give in service to others in need. Souls want to wrap their blankets of healing energy around their egos and say, "Come home to me so that I can care for you and remind you of what actually matters in your human experience." Are you willing to know the real mission of your Soul and step out of exhaustion, people pleasing, chasing money, and sacrifice? There is a sanctuary in your creativity garden where the answer of why you are here can be found, and the answer changes as you grow and evolve.

Is the reason you are on Earth reflected in how you earn your living and provide for your daily needs? We say that when the two become one, and your work fills you with the undiluted love of the Central Sun, then you have stepped into the grandness of the Heaven within you. However, if you discover that the way you pay for your living expenses is not what Soul wishes for you to experience, trust yourself and keep moving forward. It does not mean that something is wrong with you or that you are not hearing the mission of your Soul. It says that you are multitasking and that you have things to experience while Soul also has an agenda of what it needs to express through you. What if your work does fill your life with joy and a sense of purpose, yet your humanity is still longing for more balance and freedom from responsibility? The answer for this is also to be found in the sanctuary of Heart.

Trust nurtures the ego and helps you balance the demands of everyday life with fulfilling the mission of Soul. As the ego learns to let go of control, the divine nectar of God flows to your ego from your divine inner child, divine feminine, and divine masculine. In this openness of mind, Trust, grace, and balance automatically flow into your reality from Source. You don't need to do anything to make this happen. Living the mission of Soul, while being a happy human being, can be beautiful when your personality no longer resists what Soul is bringing you to experience.

Are you ready to enter the sanctuary of Soul and ask the questions that the ego needs to ask? Does Soul want you to live a lack-free life? Is your time to do this now? Does Soul aim to have your day job be the same as your happiest spiritual service work? Does Soul want you to experience mental, emotional, and physical health? Your divine inner child is looking forward to receiving your full attention so that you can hear the answers and trust them.

Healing Experience
Entering the Sanctuary of Soul

Close your eyes and breathe deeply and peacefully. Step up to the purple door and sound the alarm to clear the old male and old female waiting to distract you from entering the sanctuary.

Touch the crystal doorknob of the purple door and say, "Take me Home, divine inner child." The door opens into the most beautiful world you have ever seen. The colors are extra vibrant. The air is turquoise blue, fresh and clear. You can hear a brook gently singing and everything is fragrant.

Your divine inner child takes you by the hand, and you walk together on a path lit with golden leaves and pine needles. You walk together through an archway of white, yellow, and red thornless roses. The light is so bright, you can only trust the wise leader guiding you.

You hear bells ringing softly and kind voices whispering they love you. Your divine inner child asks you to sit in the most comfortable and plush ruby recliner that you have ever experienced. And gradually your inner eye adjusts to the brightness, and you see, know, sense, and feel your Helpers in Heaven.

Your divine feminine, divine masculine, and nature Angel of your physical body are also present. Say, "I surrender to living my highest vibrational and most joyful life. I surrender to the calling of my Soul, and I thank you for moving any resistance out of my way."

Enjoy listening to your Helpers in Heaven. Their messages will be integrated into your intuitive thought. Trust that you will know all that is beneficial for you to know.

Once the meeting is complete, you will find yourself on the other side of the purple door, thinking about your day and the tasks before you.

In a few days, or when you feel ready to return to the sanctuary of Soul, ask the Helpers, "What do I need to allow myself to receive into my earthly movie that benefits all?"

Having confidence that you are living the mission of your Soul improves all things in daily life, even your mental, emotional, and physical health. If health and balance are lacking then we ask you not to judge your humanity but to release the fear held within so that you can stay on track, full Heart Power ahead!

Mental, Emotional, and Physical Health

When health is seriously compromised, there is a story of compounded fear, despair, suffering, and rage stuck in the cellular memory. To support your health, we ask that you value the effort it takes to feel your feelings and free your mind and body of the deep subconscious, lowest vibration emotions as well as unpleasant feelings you find yourself processing currently. If you have great health then thank your body often and if your health is subpar then thank your body for helping you to understand the emotional messages it is relaying to the ego.

Emotion, at the vibration of love, forgiveness, compassion, and gratitude, always benefits the healing of your physical body and helps your mental body rebalance the brain chemicals needed for excellent functioning. When the lowest vibration emotions, such as resentment, rage, self-loathing, and guilt, are ignored or rejected, they go underground into your subconscious and eventually into your cellular subconscious. Here they hide and fester until they have grown into an internal volcano of emotional neglect and surface as a health crisis. Low vibration emotions can be inherited through the family lineage and brought in from past lives. From our perspective, all cancers, genetic diseases, and chronic illnesses have either an underlying family linage of lowest vibration emotions, or there is a past life lineage of toxic stories trapped in the cells.

Our message to you is that undiluted love is the greatest healing Power. We are not telling you to stop seeing your highly skilled and knowing physicians. However, there is something that you can do to add to their excellent knowledge and help support your health and well-being. It all starts with the ego being willing to listen to your body and respect it for the profoundly wise spiritual messenger that it is. The human body is all knowing and all powerful in its ability to live, die, or exist in a state between living and dying. If health is missing, love is missing. If disease, anxiety, pain, or problems are plaguing you, fear's archetypes of the old male and old female are renting your real estate, and you need to evict them. To help you understand, we have provided below a partial list of prevalent health concerns and their emotional and life-story origins (which can be inherited). Following the list is a healing experience that will benefit wellness and promote healing. Our exercise does not replace the need for advice from healing practitioners whom your intuition and common sense confirm you can trust and respect. Asking for help for your body is loving your body. Acknowledging your feelings is also loving your body.

▶ **List of Health Concerns and Their Underlying Roots**
- **Bone disease:** compromising of one's truth; slavery; punishment; hunger
- **Cancers:** guilt; shame; blame; loss; sorrow; blocked creativity; hatred of self or another; abuse; victim consciousness; and control
- **Dementia, Alzheimer's, Parkinson's, short-term memory loss, stroke:** stress; anxiety; fear; the need to be in control; a dominant masculine-ego mind
- **Depression:** fear; stress; anxiety; loneliness; self-rejection; repression of needs
- **Diabetes and pancreas disease:** lack of affection; emotional or physical neglect; lack of attention especially from one of the parents

- **Digestive or eating disorders:** stress; absorbing emotions from others; fear of being hurt emotionally or physically; psychic overwhelm and distress; management of self-rejection; need for self-punishment; fear of lack
- **Drug or alcohol use or any type of addiction:** self-medicating bipolar disorder, anxiety, depression, or other mental imbalances; emotional overwhelm; social anxiety; management of self-loathing; loneliness; abandonment of one's creativity garden
- **Heart disease:** difficulty in trusting self or others; difficulty in receiving or giving or both; difficulty in feeling one's emotions and releasing them
- **Kidney disease:** abandoned or neglected child within; child needing to absorb emotions for the parent; stress; loud, abusive, or frightening childhood environment
- **Liver and gallbladder disease:** rage; victimization; frustration; abuse; trauma
- **Lung disease:** sorrow; loss; anguish; grief; despair
- **Reproductive organ disease:** blocked or repressed creativity; sexual abuse; incest
- **Thyroid disease:** loss of will; self-sacrifice; stress; overwhelm of responsibility

To be willing to release the stuck fear and forgive the old stories is very helpful as it tells your body that you have received the messages given to you through the body's messaging system of pain, inflammation, and sensation. Doing our next healing experience will, in time, make it easier to hear what your body is communicating. Undiluted love is a powerful healing tonic that is good for your adrenals and helps your mental, emotional, and physical body to recover from injury and the stresses of life. Please read through this exercise before calling in the Angel Love Doctors.

Healing Experience
Healing Session with the
Angel Physicians

Lie down on your bed and get comfortable for a nap. Close your eyes and take a deep breath in and exhale completely. Your healing session will last thirty to forty-five minutes.

See yourself floating in an emerald, white, and gold energy field of singing light. Say, "I invite the Angel Love Doctors into my field. I invite my divine inner child, divine feminine, divine masculine, and the nature Angel of my body into this sacred space."

Describe to your team of Helpers in Heaven what you are feeling emotionally and physically. Share your concerns and thoughts with them. Repeat, "Thank you, Helpers and Healers, for this healing session. I release all the fear that I am holding in my mental, emotional, and physical bodies. I forgive all the toxic stories even if I don't know what they are. I forgive it all. I thank you for saturating my body with undiluted love."

Lie still and rest or sleep. The Angel Love Doctors will awaken you when your healing session ends.

Being creative, in thought or action, is good for your health. Another suggestion to support bringing in energy and wellness where it is lacking is to go outside, find a tree that calls to you, and put your back up against it. Send your energy down into the earth and hug the roots of the tree. Say, "Thank you, kind tree Angel, for grounding me to the Heart of Archangel Gaia. I am so grateful to receive from Mother Nature." Stay rooted until the tree releases you. This will take less than five minutes and if you wish, turn around, face the tree, and give it a warm hug from the Heart.

We offer you a gift for having sessions with the Angel Love Doctors. Every healing session that you request benefits other human beings that the Angels reach through the vibration of your subconscious stories. Our gift is to tell you how to enjoy a peaceful passing into Heaven when it is time for Soul to take you Home and return your body to Mother Earth. Please read through the healing experience and know that reading it will not influence when you die. By doing this exercise now, you help the ego feel positive about surrendering completely to Soul and crossing the rainbow bridge to Heaven at the time of death. The Angel of Death will visit you for a few months to a few years before it is time for you to exit Schoolroom Earth. She is a most beautiful Angel, and you will feel her loving-kindness and safety when she is present.

Healing Experience
Graceful Exit from the Dance Floor

Close your eyes and say, "I surrender fully to the love and care of my Soul." Touch the crystal doorknob of the purple door and say, "Take me Home, divine inner child." Your divine inner child leads you to the sanctuary of Soul and puts your ruby recliner in the full recline position.

You begin to see loved ones in Heaven. They look young and friendly, so happy to visit with you. Your divine feminine and divine masculine are there too. Say, "When my time comes to leave my body and cross the rainbow bridge, please come get me so that I do not resist this great liberation. I Am willing to experience the miracle of a joyful and serene passing from this world into Heaven."

Your Helpers in Heaven will put you under a violet-fire rain shower and then push your recliner, like a canoe, out a golden passageway into the violet-fire ocean of transformation and forgiveness.

We use our Sound and Light to release from your deepest subconscious any stories of traumatic death or drawn-out dying with suffering. Say, "I release all stories of unpleasant or painful deaths held in my cellular memory and give them to Creator. I forgive these old stories even though I do not remember them." Once the fear has been cleared from your vessel, the ocean will turn into a rainbow of colors, and the energy will fill you with unconditional love and overflowing respect for your humanity and for the divinity that is your immortal Self.

We will lift you out of the rainbow sea and gently ground you back in the present so that you can continue with your day.

Doing this exercise will also help the ego to adapt to change so that you continue to evolve in consciousness all your days and beyond. Inner peacefulness is immeasurable and as you feel safer in your human skin, lack must leave and make room for wealth.

Respecting that we have given you our finest and most effective tools to bring undiluted love where it has been missing, we now ask you to help us. Within you lives the human collective and although you may be receiving more Heaven by the minute, much of the One Human Body is dead asleep to knowing about the Power of undiluted love. Will you help us to reach the lost and disconnected egos that are drowning in disrespect of their humanity and projecting this disrespect and self-rejection onto others? Will you help us reach those who are in despair and suffering? And will you help us reach those who are misusing their power and creating destruction for the inhabitants of your one-of-a-kind blue planet? Will you be a vehicle for positive change? We thank you, great Being of God's Sound and Light, for acting as a healing Angel for Schoolroom Earth!

Peace and Balance
So Within, So Without

You are the superhero that can help us reinstate peace and balance on Earth when you join forces with your divine inner child and allow your divinity to flow through every cell of you. How is this possible? Your wise and incredible Soul is living through you and through other personalities in the human collective at the same time. We call these other personalities your "parallel lives."

Have you ever had a dream where you were someone else, living somewhere else, and the dream felt so real that when you woke up, you were surprised to be in the life you are living? All these dream lives, together with your past lives, and the experiences of your ancestors are stories that you can access through your subconscious. Can you comprehend the number of generations that live within you, the parallel lives that connect with this life, and all the past lives of these parallel lives together with the past lives that you have felt glimpses of in this life? Your stories, from the present and past, provide vibrational pathways to send healing out to those in need of undiluted love. The 12 Archangels of the Central Sun, together with the Ascended Masters and Helpers in Heaven, need to reach those suffering and disconnected egos through the vast libraries of beliefs, thoughts, memories, and feelings that can be accessed through YOU.

We ask that you join us in bringing love to the disturbing movies of

Schoolroom Earth that desperately need a vibrational shift out of fear. We ask that you use the divine laws to give your own humanity a vibrational super shift and from there, together, we can send healing energy to where transformation is needed. Let us show you how this works for your greatest good and the greatest good of all concerned. We begin by asking you to help us to flood your schoolroom with peace and balance. As the undiluted love flows into the negative strife of internal conflict between your wounded ego and Soul, disharmony rises to be transformed. Because of the divine Law of As Above, So Below, As Within, So Without, together with our help, you become a powerful transformer of conflict in the global movie. Please read through this deepest healing exercise slowly and continue to read it until you can sense the peace flowing into your cells and disharmony being pushed up and out. We are in this with you, lifting the fear, conflict, and imbalance to the Central Sun.

Healing Experience
Bringing Peace and Balance to Earth

Close your eyes and breathe slowly until you feel centered and secure. Step through the purple door into a coral landscape. Once you enter the coral world, say, "I invite my being to be rebalanced by my Soul."

Just ahead of you are two huge piles of black sand. The pile on the right is bigger than the pile on the left. When you look around, you notice that there are six palm trees growing in the coral landscape and all of them are on the left. There seems to be nothing growing on the right. The rest of the landscape is barren, like dried-out, red-orange mud.

Place your hands on your abdomen and say, "Fear out, love in." See your divine inner child, divine feminine, and divine masculine pouring violet-fire water on the black sand pile. They are pouring the energy on the line that has been drawn in the middle of the sand. Keep repeating, "Fear out, love in."

Soon you will feel and see that the sand is disappearing. Say, "Peace in, conflict out." Keep your hands relaxed on your abdomen and take deep breaths, pushing your belly into your hands when you inhale. The black sand completely disappears. Watch as the palm trees spread over the coral landscape and now grow on the right side as well as the left.

Say, "Thank you, Creator, for filling my humanity with peace and balance for the greatest good and the highest joy of all!"

The coral landscape is being filled with vegetation and flowers of many colors. A beautiful Angel appears. Say, "Thank you, Archangel Gaia, for rebalancing your planet. Thank you for helping me to rebalance my body and my life. Thank you for transforming the self-hatred of your children into love and respect for one another. I Am so grateful."

Stand under a violet-fire waterfall and release any selves from your past that still feel conflicted or bitter. Say, "I forgive it all, even if I don't want to forgive it. I invite peace and balance to fill my being and the One Human Body that I live within."

Invite the violet-fire waterfall to transform into a rainbow vortex of undiluted love. Stand in the vortex and become the vortex of love. Grow until you are vast. Feel our energy merge with you. From this place of unity and Divine Oneness, we send peace, balance, and respect into the atoms of every particle of Creator's energy on Earth. As above, so below and as within, so without, obeying the Law of One and the Law of Energy.

We would like to interpret the symbolic language that we use in this exercise. The coral landscape represents your second, or Soul, chakra located around your belly button area. By asking you to focus on this chakra, we can reach all Souls and their human expressions through your Soul. The black grains of sand represent conflict between the ego and Soul, negative and resentful thoughts, unsettled feelings, and painful memories of victimization. They are also symbolic of time. The past will repeat itself in the future if the fear has not been transformed. The black color of the sand represents both fear and the potential energy locked in the fear. The six (number of love) growing palm trees represent fresh air, protection, nurturing, growing life, and creativity. In the beginning of the exercise, they are all on the left, which is symbolic of the feminine. When the trees move, some remain on the left and some move to the right, balancing the feminine with the masculine. Nature is constantly rebalancing and healing you. The vegetation and flowers represent love, beauty, harmony, and healing.

We asked you to breathe into your belly. Your belly holds the Great Universe in the mirror of all the microbes that live within you, helping you to digest your emotions and your food to keep you alive. Coconut oil from the coconuts of the palm trees will kill parasites (symbolic of fear that feeds off fear) in your gut. This part of the exercise creates balance within you and automatically sends balance and health out into the cells of the One Human Body. We complete the exercise by having your ego forgive perceived mistakes from the past that might still cause anxiety. Violet fire transforms fear (guilt, shame, and blame) into love. Merging with the rainbow vortex of undiluted love fills you with inner peace. Your inner peace multiplies and flows from the oneness we create out to the collective and to all of Earth.

Each time you complete this healing experience, know that your human self is a peaceful and balanced cell in the body of the One Human Body. The cell that is you is now communicating with all the other cells in the One Human Body and raising the vibration of the other cells. This naturally encourages them to let go of conflict and fill up with peace.

See how all three divine laws are working through you as you do our healing experience. You have used the singing colors of the rays of the Central Sun to raise the vibration of your energy (Law of Energy). With your hands on your belly, you have called on the Law of One and by doing the exercise with us, we have enacted the Law of As Above, So Below, As Within, So Without.

We have more joyful missions of transformation and healing to do with you. YOU are as powerful as an Archangel, and together we can move Schoolroom Earth out of lack and into balance. Let's do it!

PART 6

Moving Schoolroom
Earth Out of Suffering

We merge our Heart Power with yours. Together, we heal the One Human Body and the planet on which you live and learn.

THE 12 ARCHANGELS OF THE CENTRAL SUN

Transforming Poverty

Poverty is the outer reflection of the One Human Body being disconnected from Divine Mother's love, safety, and security. Along with reconnecting humanity to Source, ending poverty necessitates the clearing of fear's old female. She makes you want to hold on to the loss experienced in the past and see yourself as a victim of unchangeable circumstances. First, we will assist you in your own deepest clearing and healing, and then through you, we will facilitate the transformation of poverty on Schoolroom Earth.

Let's enter the library of your beliefs where we use the metaphor of stories recorded in books for releasing limiting, fear-based belief paradigms. Some of these beliefs belong to your parents and were passed on to you during childhood. Some of these beliefs you adopted during times of hardship and crisis in your own life. We ask you to consider these stories as moldy and toxic, not full of sage wisdom to keep you safe from thieves during hard times. Once we assist you in clearing these old female beliefs stored in the memory rooms of the upper subconscious, we will travel deep into the violet-fire ocean to transform the ancient stories of loss experienced by your ancestors and past-life selves.

Healing Experience

Letting Go of Fear's Old Female Poverty Beliefs

Close your eyes and take in a deep breath of love. Exhale any fear that you feel. Step through the purple door, climb the stairs to your library of beliefs. Make sure to turn on the violet-fire sprinkler system that is just above the potted plants in the corner of the entry. You can be sure that the old male and old female are anticipating your visit, and they will surely want to distract you from your mission of letting go of poverty and victim consciousness.

In the middle of the main library, the 12 Archangels stand together with your guardian Angels, divine inner child, divine feminine, and divine masculine. We have piled all the books that need to be transformed. Feel free to sort through the books yourself; however, we give you warning that each book is full of sad stories of loss, hunger, shortage, hardship, and suffering.

We have already installed a violet-fire conveyor belt that runs from the table with the pile of books to the Central Sun. All the low vibration energy stuck in the books will be recycled, transformed into love, and returned to you.

Say, "I release, and I let go of all the victim consciousness wrapped in my stories of hardship, struggle, and loss. I release all the trapped energy in the memories, whether they are my memories, or things I have absorbed from listening to the hardship stories of others."

Watch all the books from the table move up the conveyor belt, out through the opening in the roof, and on up to the infinite singing light of the golden Central Sun.

Archangels Michael and Victoria offer you a sapphire blue and white-fire Sword of Truth, Justice, and Victory. Sitting on a chair at the head of the large table is a huge book with the title, *Poverty and Hardship Purifies You in the Eyes of God.* Take the Sword of Truth from the Angels and pierce the book all the way through. It will turn into dust and the Angels will blow the dust to the Central Sun.

Check your library for old males and old females and if any are found, put them on the conveyor belt and send them straight to God's energy recycler. Say, "I Am abundant and always provided for by Source. I Am part of Divine Oneness. Divine Oneness can experience only abundance and plenty."

◇◇◇

Rest before reading through our next healing experience. If you prefer, do this exercise at bedtime to allow the Angels to do a thorough scrubbing of your DNA molecules and cellular subconscious.

Healing Experience
Transforming Poverty from the Inside Out

Close your eyes and breathe peacefully. Touch the crystal doorknob of the purple door and say, "I am willing to be of service to Divine Oneness. I am willing to be free of fear, poverty, hardship, pain, and suffering. I do this healing for the greatest good of all concerned."

Open the door and swim with your divine inner child out into the middle of the violet-fire ocean. Your way is lit with golden sparkling stars that are fun to eat because they are made of the highest vibrational chocolate.

You will see us, 12 pillars of loving light, waiting for you. Take a seat in the ruby recliner made of Divine Mother's love. Say, "I release all stories of loss held within my vessel."

We call out of your cellular subconscious and DNA memory vaults stories of the following:

- Death, abandonment, or neglect by financial providers
- War, slavery, or inhumane working conditions
- Being an unmarried mother or jobless parent or being unable to support yourself, your children, or both

- Loss of crops, loss of limbs, loss of mental stability or ability, and loss of personal power
- Loss of motivation, inspiration, and the energy to move forward in life
- Hunger, food shortage, or poor nutrition
- Loss due to addiction, depression, or poor health
- Loss of homeland, property and resources, or family
- Work required being far more than the income provided
- Financial shortage
- Job loss or a career change that comes with disruption
- Loss of faith in Creator, especially in the loss of receiving from the Divine Mother
- Loss of trust and belief in yourself and in your creative intelligence
- Loss of respect for yourself leading to the belief that Soul must have abandoned you
- Fear of poverty, hardship, or lack of having resources in the future

Repeat, "I forgive these old stories for all of us. I forgive them even if they feel unforgivable." Do this until you feel light and calm. The past experiences of poverty that weigh down your subconscious are now on their way to the Central Sun!

And now, from your peaceful vessel, we call out all the suffering and struggling selves, and we carry them gently to the Central Sun. Say, "Thank you, Mother-Father-God, for filling all my suffering and struggling selves including my past lives and ancestors with overflowing compassion and healing. Thank you for transforming the lower vibrations of fear and sadness into love and joy. I call this transformed and renewed energy into my being with love, gratitude, and respect for all."

The image of the violet-fire ocean disappears and now you see the emerald field of Heart. We invite you to say with us, "I Am willing to help the human collective! I Am willing to help Mother Earth!"

You are now a leaf on a giant tree. The tree represents the entire human collective. Feel the roots of this tree pushing deeper into the Earth until they enter the Heart of Archangel Gaia. The roots light up in emerald and gold and begin to hum. Your leaf can feel the rhythm of this magnificent tree.

Once the roots fully connect with Heart, the humming emerald and gold energy swiftly moves up the roots, into the trunk and branches. The leaves start to dance in the wind and light up in the colors of the rainbow. The singing light from the Central Sun is filling each leaf on the tree with eternal abundance, while the roots absorb everlasting nurturance.

Say, "We are all one and we are all fed all we need."'

Open your Heart Power, connect with our Hearts, and feel our energy merge with you. From this place of unity and oneness, we send true wealth and balance into the atoms of every struggling being of Creator's energy. Through the Law of One and the Law of As Above, So Below, As Within, So Without, we give thanks that this is so.

Transforming global poverty goes hand in hand with transforming global homelessness. All Souls that enter Schoolroom Earth carry the feeling of being exiled from Heaven's eternal grace and freedom. The vibrational difference between the Great Universe and Earth can seem extreme. When the human expression of a star Soul encounters fear for the first time, it can be so overwhelming that the personality can believe they are destitute and must fight for survival as early as infancy. Until your humanity fully unites with your divinity so that the ego is securely nourished by the Trust of Heart, you may feel lost and homeless at different times. Some humans take on the story of being exiled from their home countries or families to facilitate healing for the One Human Body.

The fear of being forced to abandon one's home for any reason is powerful in its effect on the global community. It contributes to competition for resources, greed, the misuse of power, and violence. Our next mission is to transform the fear of exile and homelessness and to bring an end to this trauma, for the greatest good of all.

Transforming Exile
and Homelessness

The story of exile and the profound trauma that it creates has ancient roots in the memory of the human collective. Exile can happen for a multitude of reasons—extreme weather, politics, religious persecution, poverty, and abandonment to name a few. Whatever the reason for uprooting one's life and changing environments, the lasting shock, grief, rage, and fear is worthy of transformation. As you transform from your cellular memory and nervous system the underground fear that the past will repeat, you help yourself and future generations. Another more subtle form of the fear of exile and homelessness is the fear of contracting an incurable disease where you no longer feel safe in your body.

Fearing that your body might abandon you or that an unpredictable change may leave you homeless is food for the old male and old female. This fear of dramatic change originates from believing that God has abandoned you or that your family members, community, or tribe have abandoned you. When the experience of abandonment is part of your history, it is like walking on a fault line because subconsciously, you are always bracing for disaster. Ultimately, trusting that all experiences are designed to bring you home to your Heart can transform the negative potential of exile. Raising your vibration and surrendering to the undiluted love of Soul will carry you through life's lessons with much less trauma and displacement. To help keep your vibration as free of fear as possible, we will help you clear the root cause of experiencing the need to flee to save your life, sanity, children, or values.

Our first step is to encourage you to thank the Divine Mother and Mother Earth for supplying you with a safe home and body, especially if you do not currently feel safe. Gratitude is a positive super shifter for your vibration. As your vibration goes up, it is easier for you to receive what you need to thrive in your life. As you are helped, all benefit.

Our second step is to ask that you stay aware of the old male and old female bullying you with disaster-prevention strategies. The future is not here yet. Put your energy into creating a future that feels even more safe, harmonious, and lovely than the one you are currently experiencing.

Our third step is to ask that you do the following healing experience to transform the painful stories of your ancestors. Repeat as needed when you worry about your safety and security.

Healing Experience
Violet Fire for Releasing the Trauma of Exile

Close your eyes and see yourself as an erupting volcano releasing violet-fire lava. The lava symbolizes buried anger that needs to rise to the surface. Transform the rage into love using the power of forgiveness. Say, "I willingly release the anger and shock of my ancestors and past-life selves." Allow the volcano to erupt until the lava stops, and the scene changes to a violet ocean.

You are together with your divine inner child, resting comfortably in a ruby chair. We surround you in the ocean and appear as 12 giant pillars of singing color. We are singing to your human cells and asking them to release all family tragedies. Release the emotions surrounding your family's belief that they were invisible to Creator.

We now sing out of your cells all fear concerning feeling valued, safe, secure, and provided for by Source. We invite you to bring the violet color into your skin so that you feel the power of forgiveness reach your molecules and atoms. Say, "I forgive it all. I forgive that which is unforgivable. I forgive it for all concerned."

And when all is clear, we change the scene to the sanctuary of Soul in the emerald world of Heart. This is your true Home that can never be taken from you, not even in death.

From the sanctuary of Soul, open your Heart Power, connect with our Hearts, and feel our energy merge with you. From this place of unity, we send the vibration of Home into the atoms of everyone who is struggling. Through the Law of Energy, the Law of One, and the Law of As Above, So Below, As Within, So Without, we give thanks that this is so.

Our next mission for you, most brave and willing world healer, is to transform the story of the abandonment, neglect, disrespect, and abuse of children. We include pets because pets mirror the wounded child to their owner and absorb suffering for them. Using the greatest Power of undiluted love, you can make a significant difference in ending the patterns of abuse that continue to repeat generation after generation. Let us spread our wings, connect with Divine Oneness, and change what may appear to be impossible to change!

Transforming Neglect and Abuse of Children

Did you know that in Heaven you can be a child, teenager, young adult, or adult depending on your mood? Have you ever asked yourself the question, "Why are childhood and parenting part of the already intense education on Schoolroom Earth?" These experiences are instrumental in learning the value of being an immortal, all-loving, and all-forgiving divine child. Let us help you to understand, from a place of divine compassion, what happens when you incarnate on Earth, and why life can begin as a huge disappointment.

On Schoolroom Earth, personalities get disconnected from the ever-flowing fountain of guidance and love of the true mother and father of Soul. Allowing this Truth to soak in, you can begin to realize that it is not possible for any human parent to sustain the unconditional love of the Divine Mother and Father of the Great Universe. Divine, unconditional love is exactly what a new baby wants from their human parents. The newly incarnated Soul has left the vibration of Heaven and entered the dense, fear-saturated reality of Earth. Immediately the new baby discovers that their parents are human, fragile, broken, and needy children. The infant that has just gone through the experience of birth looks into the eyes of their mother and says, "I know you. We agreed to be in this movie together, and I want to help you." The mother, whether the birth mother or the surrogate mother, looks into the eyes of her infant

178

and says, "I want to give you everything!" The new mother may not understand that she can only give what she is able to give, and she may feel defeated with her recognition that she cannot give enough. When the mother already has several children, she may be asking, "How am I going to care for another one when I am already exhausted?"

The experiences for both the parent and the child can be a movie with sad and shocking scenes. Without undiluted love and forgiveness, entire lives may continue to be full of pain and shame because of what transpires in infancy, early childhood, and the teenage years. The pain from childhood can then be acted out on others, even pets. In this situation, the original pain has multiplied and feels even heavier with the addition of guilt, shame, and blame. How can the low vibrations of neglect, abandonment, and abuse be understood, forgiven, and transformed? Asking for help from wise counselors and asking for healing from Soul can work miracles in helping all concerned to understand the root causes of the suffering. We recommend that all human personalities do just this: ask for their Souls to intervene and stop the pain. You may not be able to change the suffering of someone else; however, you can make a request of their Soul for a divine intervention on their behalf. It helps to come from a place of real compassion for all parties caught in the cycle of neglect or abuse. Compassion needs to be from the Heart. Let us help you to develop a greater understanding of abuse.

Human parents are often blind to their subconscious projection of their own self-rejection and hurt onto their children. Without knowing it, they can take out their self-loathing on the innocent and vulnerable. Pet owners can have a similar lack of awareness and project negative emotions onto their furry companions. Forgiveness for all of it, especially that which feels unforgivable, is the solution.

It may help to understand that Souls design their traumatic childhood stories before they incarnate. Major violations of boundaries are agreed to on a Soul level and prior to entering Schoolroom Earth. The hopeful news is that all agreements between the abuser and victim can be changed prior to the traumatic event. Abuse can be stopped! How? By self-forgiveness entering the consciousness of the abuser, and the Power of undiluted love flooding the victim. Let us explain. In the case where a parent was abused as a child, their child may take on a similar experience to help the parent remember their own trauma and heal. The adult who is misusing their power over a child, or pet, is projecting onto the child what repeatedly happened to them in this life or a recent past life. When such an adult clears fear's old male and old female so that they can reparent their own wounded children within them, they transform being both the victim and the abuser. Children who have brought in the residue of a violent past life can also be the abuser of their parents, other family members, and pets. No matter where the story of abuse began, it deserves to be transformed with the phenomenal healing power of forgiveness.

The ultimate lesson is to forgive even that which feels unforgivable and to see the abuser as the wounded and broken personality that is functioning the best they can function, which may not be at all. Within every abusive human being is a trampled child who is screaming to be heard. For the one who is hurting, a team of Angels stand watch and will intercede on the command of Soul.

Please allow Archangels Michael and Victoria to wrap you in a force field of courage as you look at the following list of feelings and behaviors associated with abuse. Be sure to notice when any feeling or behavior resonates with you. Confirmation of your feelings could come through the contraction of your breath or discomfort in your physical body. Please note that our list is vibrational and may not include your exact feelings.

▶ **Feelings and Behaviors Associated with Abuse**
- Unpredictable bad mood or temper when things feel out of control
- Anxiety

- Sorrow
- Unworthiness that is difficult to shake
- Shame
- Guilt
- Road rage
- Weak boundaries
- Nightmares
- Unexplained exhaustion
- Hypersensitivity with respect to environment and strangers
- Strong desire to predict the future and control it if possible
- Difficulty in respecting your own needs as much as you do the needs of others
- Difficulty in making a decision
- Difficulty in getting enough money to cover your needs
- Frequent need for approval
- Strong negative judgment of your physical body
- Shame around spending money on yourself
- Fear of asking for help
- Fear of taking a risk
- Fear of seeking medical advice when medical help is needed
- Fear of being alone
- Fear of being with strangers
- Fear of affection
- Fear of emotional intimacy
- Fear of sexual intimacy
- Fear of feeling your feelings and expressing your needs, even to yourself
- Feeling not good enough
- Judging others who have acted disrespectfully
- Judging or criticizing another for being different than yourself
- Feeling under pressure
- Feeling that something must be wrong with you

- Uncomfortable receiving, more comfortable giving
- Reacting to challenging situations in life by feeling victimized, cheated, and resentful
- Yelling, cursing, or verbally disrespecting the space of another
- Putting another person down
- Directing sarcasm at others
- Punishing self, children, or animals
- Competing for attention
- Dissociating or stepping out of yourself
- Having addictions and strong attachments to activities, drugs, money, alcohol, sex, or anything harmful to yourself or to another
- Needing to be the center of attention or the opposite, needs to be the giver of attention, not the receiver
- Needing to be in control and hold the power to feel safe
- Parenting all or just the needy one who is often in crisis
- Preferring to accommodate the choices of others and avoid conflict

Healing Experience
Forgiving the Traumas of Childhood

Close your eyes and breathe in. Your Soul, divine inner child, divine feminine, divine masculine, and the nature Angel of your body are helping you to recognize what is ripe to be forgiven.

Wrap any resonating feelings or behaviors from the list above in violet fire and place the packages on the emerald ground next to you. Say, "I surrender my childhood to the healing of Soul, united with the Central Sun. I forgive all hurtful events, whether obvious traumas or subtle ones. I forgive all the characters in the movie of my childhood even if it feels difficult to forgive them. And I forgive myself, and I forgive Divine Oneness for feeling abandoned by God."

Take the packages lying on the emerald ground and place them on the turquoise and gold conveyor belt that is pointed toward the heavens. We promise to deliver each special package to Creator for you. Say, "I invite Soul to fill me with freedom and joy!"

It is now time to dive deep and clear abuse from your genetics. Doing so helps you, helps your family, and greatly helps the human collective.

Healing Experience
DNA Scrub for Clearing Neglect and Abuse

Please read through the exercise and if preferred, ask for your guardian Angels and Helpers in Heaven to do the clearing while you sleep at night.

Take a few deep breaths. Continue until you feel calm and grounded. Walk through the open purple door and jump into the violet-fire ocean with sparkling golden stars. Swim with your divine inner child until you reach us, a circle of 12 Angels, all in white-gold singing light.

In the middle of our circle is a large emerald disk. Please lie down upon it. It will feel comfortable and safe. We gently cover you with a soft ruby pink blanket, and we lift out of your molecules your ancestors' stories of the following:

- Incest
- Sex trafficking and prostitution at any age of life
- Molestation and sexual inappropriateness
- Physical punishment or verbal humiliation
- Psychological abuse, including psychic abuse (hearing abusive or sexually invasive thoughts through one's intuition)
- Physical hunger

- Imprisonment, confinement, or emotional enslavement
- Lack of safety, security, and stability
- Fear, rage, guilt, and shame
- Sacrifice
- Physical, mental, or emotional suffering or being witness to it
- Betrayal and manipulation by a trusted adult or advisor
- Being bullied, teased, tormented, or tortured
- Being a child laborer
- Being forced into a sport or religious or educational activity that was traumatizing
- Having to grow up too quickly to survive the family dysfunction and crisis
- Witnessing violence, destruction, and death
- Being rejected or abandoned by either parent figure
- Being separated from one's family as an infant, child, or teenager for any amount of time that caused shock in the nervous system
- Being brainwashed with fear
- Being the one who goes without while those around you have what they need

We send all these painful stories to the Central Sun. We ask that you say, "I release these tragic stories from my molecules and atoms. I release them for all of us, and I forgive them even if they are unforgivable." Repeat, "I FORGIVE" until you feel lighter, and the violet of the ocean changes to the colors of a rainbow.

We lift you off the disk in the rainbow ocean and place you on the emerald ground of Heart. Your ruby pink blanket soaks into your body and is quickly replaced by a new blanket. The blankets of energy continue to soak into your being until you are fully saturated with innocence and undiluted love from the Divine Mother of the Great Universe.

Say, "Thank you, Divine Mother, for helping me to receive into my human atoms the vibration of a new and happy childhood. I Am willing for you to be my mother and for the Divine Father to be my father."

Your divine feminine and masculine take a glowing yellow ball of the highest vibrational self-esteem energy and place it in your solar plexus. The confidence grows and fills every cell of your humanity with the self-worth of your divinity. Say, "I Am human fully divine and divine fully human!"

We, the 12 Archangels, now merge our energy with your energy. Together we call on all the star beings of the Great Universe to add their Heart Power to this magical fusion. We send this happy-childhood re-creation LOVE into the moment of conception, past, present, and future of all human beings to continue to facilitate freedom and healing. We also send this re-creation and ascension energy into all the atoms existing on the Earth and into the fearful vibrations of the astral filter.

Command and activate with us by saying, "All are one. All are made whole again, through the power of the divine laws and the Heart Power of Creator's undiluted love."

Transforming Hatred, Violence, and Evil with Undiluted Love

At the lowest vibration allowed on Schoolroom Earth, fear's most addictive and convincing illusion can have the ego dreaming a nightmare into reality. At this point of seemingly no return, the ego is so saturated with fear and self-loathing that it believes that love is nonexistent. In this most frightening nightmare, the ego's humanity has fallen into the darkest abyss of separation from Soul and is now feeding on fear and using fear as the power to survive the terrible dream that the ego is living. We thank you for your courage to read our words and to hear our honest plea. Will you help us orchestrate a divine rescue for those trapped in a movie where hatred, violence, or evil is a part of the scene they are experiencing, real or imagined?

Please read through the healing experience and have chocolate on hand for before and after. Chocolate is our earthly medicine for helping the brain to shift in vibration, and it is very helpful for clearing any absorption of negative or fearful thoughts. If you do not enjoy chocolate, then please request your guardian Angel to super charge the molecules of water you are drinking with the vibration of chocolate.

Healing Experience
Divine Rescue

Close your eyes and breathe in love. With your intention, exhale all fear from your body. Breathe in more love in your favorite colors of the singing rays of the Central Sun.

Walk through the purple door and find Archangels Michael and Metatron waiting for you at the edge of a vast, pitch-dark abyss. The hole looks and feels bottomless. Take the hand of your divine inner child and watch as huge and gentle sapphire blue wings of undiluted love wrap around you. Say, "I Am willing to help the most cancerous cells in the One Human Body. Yes, I Am WILLING!"

And all together you jump into the abyss. You fall like you will never reach the bottom, but you do and the landing is soft.

The Angels point in the direction of three dungeon cells, lit with a glaring orange light. In the first cell there is a male monster, in the second cell there is a female monster, and in the third cell there is a child monster. We do not ask for you to see the monsters. We do tell you that they used to look like beautiful and intelligent human beings.

Together with your divine inner child please say, "All is forgiven." The Angels shower the dungeon cells with white and violet singing light from above and send in a flood of undiluted love through the floor of each cell. Proclaim, "Love is the Source that lifts your vibration from the deepest fear to the highest frequency, undiluted love. We send you to the Central Sun."

Archangel Metatron takes the lantern with the strange orange light (symbolic for Soul, which feels so far away) and tosses it out of the abyss, back to Divine Oneness.

Angels of all shapes and sizes arrive in the abyss and with violet-fire vacuum cleaners and scrub brushes, they clear the space of fear and fear's illusion of separation.

From above, the Archangels bring in rays of undiluted love from the

Central Sun and fill the abyss. You and your divine inner child rise back to ground level and return to the emerald meadow. The abyss closes completely and ever-blossoming cherry trees appear on the scar of the closure.

Say, "I give thanks that all hate, violence, illusions of evil, and crimes of revenge and destruction are transformed, completely and totally, with undiluted love. Through Heart Power, I allow the divine laws to work through me to eradicate this heartache from Schoolroom Earth. I am thankful, Creator, that the One Human Body, of which I am a cell, is healing for the greatest good and highest joy of all."

Transforming Inequality, Racism, and Discrimination

Mother Earth welcomes Souls from all over the infinite and beautiful Great Universe to incarnate through her womb. All human beings share the same mother, and the colors of her skin can be found in her rich and fertile soil, white-sand beaches, and red-rock canyons. Tunnel walls and exposed cliffs of her impressive mountain ranges reveal an entire rainbow of shades. Can you recognize the color of your skin in the skin of Mother Earth? Whether you are as dark as her night sky and depths of her oceans or as fair as a pearl in her oysters, do you see that she is your mother, and you share her beauty and intelligence?

Your luscious blue planet is Archangel Gaia and she and her moon belong to the family of the 12 Archangels. We appreciate every Soul that visits Schoolroom Earth. No matter what their ego's education may look like, we choose to see all human beings as our siblings of Sound and Light. We share the good news that when an ego crosses the rainbow bridge at the time of physical death, any residue of racism and any kind of discrimination melts away like a pile of snow in warm summer sun. If it is true that all human beings are born from the same mother and are the siblings of the 12 Archangels, where does such vicious racism come from and what purpose does it serve?

Any personality that becomes unplugged from their Heart Power will suffer in some way or another from the lonely story of inequality. This includes the illusion that one human being is better than any other or better than an elephant or pine needle. All particles of Creator's energy are equal in their ability to shine the creative light of undiluted love. Racism and discrimination are extreme ways to learn this lesson. Unconditional acceptance of your own self is a good place to start learning what must be learned. Practice accepting, without judgment or punishment, the aspects of yourself that you detest and be a transformer of the painful reality of racism, inequality, and discrimination. The healing within you will be reflected as positive change in the "so without" of Schoolroom Earth.

What do you need to do when you are exposed to the disrespect and mistreatment of other human beings? Do you jump out of your movie and into their theater? Instead of reacting with your masculine and adding fire to the conflict, ground yourself in the emerald meadow of Heart. Say, "I Am Divine Oneness. All belong to Divine Oneness. We are Divine Oneness." As you say this short mantra, you are activating Heart Power and sending out the Truth that all are equal in the eyes of Mother-Father-God. Through your calmness, you are sending the message into the minds of all involved that God does not prefer one child over another. Through your Heart Power, you send the message to go within and transform the self-hatred that is being projected outward onto other human beings.

Discrimination begins within and is transformed from the inside out. When an ego feels inferior or superior to another, the ego has vibrationally moved away from Soul. We ask that you do not judge yourself. Do not judge the movie you are living if your life appears to be better or worse than what others are experiencing. When you add all your past lives together, you have been all colors of skin. What matters most on your long journey is that you choose to respect the divinity in all and honor that all people in the collective are siblings. Let us, the

12 Archangels, help your ego know when to plug back into Soul's Power socket and from that place of acceptance and Trust, let us merge with you and light up the living tree of the One Human Body.

Healing Experience
Transmuting the Judges

Close your eyes and take a deep breath in. Exhale completely. Walk up to the purple door and sound the old male and old female alarm to set off the violet-fire sprinkler system. Say, "OUT, OUT, OUT, controlling and judging old-male thoughts! OUT, OUT, OUT, powerless-victim and old-female feelings!"

Step through the purple door and climb the stairs to the library of beliefs. When you arrive, you notice that the library is flooded with violet fire. The violet-fire ocean, used for clearing the deep subconscious, has risen to the upper levels of the subconscious. You are experiencing a dual DNA molecular scrub and release of beliefs (books) that need to be transformed with undiluted love.

Together with your divine inner child and guardian Angel librarian, wade into the main room and ask the librarian to take you to the intimidating courtroom on the left. Here, you will find the judges of less than, equal than, and greater than holding measuring sticks and scales. The books, full of the beliefs, practices, and painful memories of your ancestors and past-life selves, are surfacing through the cracks in the floor. These books may have shocking titles such as, *Lighter Skin Is Better Than Darker Skin, Male Is Superior to Female, Older Sons Are Superior to Youngest Sons, Richer Is Better Than Poorer,* or *Jesus Is Wiser Than Mohamad.* The judges are scrambling around trying to poke the books back into the hiding places under the floor, but it is too late!

Together with your divine inner child, take the Sword of Truth from Archangel Michael's hand and place it in the middle of the courtroom. Say, "I choose the Truth of Divine Oneness to live within my mind.

Through the Power of Heart, I send all the less than, equal than, and greater than judges, beliefs, practices, and memories to the Central Sun to transform. I forgive it all even if it is unforgivable."

The courtroom blows up in an amazing blaze of violet, purple, sapphire blue, emerald, scarlet, and gold. In a blink of your inner eye, you find yourself in the emerald meadow admiring the tree of the One Human Body. A most incredible thing is happening. The emerald energy of Archangel Gaia's Heart fills the roots of the tree and continues to rise into the trunk and branches. The Central Sun fills the leaves with white-gold divine love from above and the leaves begin to dance in the wind.

The leaves at the very top of the tree move to the lowest branches and vice versa. The dance continues and with each move, the leaf that is you changes color. Yes, the color of the skin of the leaves turns every color of the rainbow on the tree of the One Human Body.

Souls are like these leaves. They enjoy changing from one incarnation to the next so that they can experience all the different perspectives of the infinite positions on the Tree of Life.

We ask that you feel a leaf that is you. Acknowledge with your ego the less than, equal than, or greater than judges in your mind. Proclaim, "I choose LOVE" and send the judges to the Central Sun.

Our energy merges with the particles of Creator's energy of the One Human Body and Mother Earth. All of us together, with you and your divine inner child, send love where it is missing. We send the Truth that all are part of Divine Oneness. We send unconditional acceptance and respect where it is missing in the One Human Body. Feel the glorious choosing of love for all. We are Divine Oneness!

Transforming Leadership and the Misuse of Power

Why do human beings believe they need to be governed, ruled, protected, and told what to do? From our perspective, only those human beings who have disconnected from their divine wisdom need or desire to follow or rebel against a leader outside of Soul. Leaders of governments, religions, institutions, corporations, and wherever else another human being seeks to lead can be divided into two primary camps. One camp uses fear's old male and old female to lead the head egos in charge. In another much smaller camp, the leader leads with their Heart Power and Soul's direction. When the leader who is leading from the ego thinks they are leading from Soul then they may deceive, manipulate, and confuse everyone, including themselves. This would be the old male and old female's favorite kind of leader because it is one who wants to have power over others so that they do their will.

Egos want instant gratification and when they have fear's old male in the driver seat, they can act from a self-righteous mindset that tells them they can have whatever they want. They believe they have the right to take it from wherever and whomever they think has it. Not only do they justify taking, but they may also enlist their followers into taking for them. What is most important for you to understand is that the best authority is always your own divine inner child, divine feminine, and divine masculine. If your ego is off track, then Soul knows how to bring you back to center so that you can live the finest life possible. Angels ask you to reclaim your own highest Will so that you use your ego power and intelligence for the greatest good of all (obeying the Law of One).

The highest vibrational law and order within you, directed by your Soul and Creator, is activated when you say, "I surrender the will of my ego to the Will of my Soul." If this does not sound impressive enough to your ego, then you may want to say, "I surrender the will of my ego to the Will of my Soul, fully united with my OverSoul." If this still does not satisfy the ego, we have one more version of a foolproof command: "I surrender the will of my ego to the Will of Source." This is a Heart Power command and is governed by all three divine laws. Saying the command will protect you from being deceived by those who direct from a wounded and disconnected ego.

Fear's old female may have seduced you into believing that you are a victim of the current and past decision makers, including your parents, coaches, schoolteachers, and medical advisors. Can every authority in your life bring disappointment and despair into your movie? We say only if you allow this to be your reality by silencing your divine Will.

Mystics have walked Schoolroom Earth for ages without being involved in conflict, held at gunpoint, or forced to go against their values and ethics to survive. They knew to keep their vibration high and fill their minds with undiluted love. They said no to being entertained by politics, judging the good from the bad, or falling prey to the sales pitch, "Follow me, do as I tell you, and I will keep you safe and rich." You have an equally powerful and wise sage living within you, and this is your divine inner child. Live your life as your Heart guides you and conflict, disaster, and loss of personal power and wealth will no longer be scenes in your movie or chapters in your story.

We are going to help you transform the selves inside who are seduced by the false promises of ego-directed leadership. Such leaders may like to use old male intimidation and old female guilt to limit the life you are living. Once your inner transformation is complete, we will offer our method for sending the highest vibrational Will to government, religious, and business leaders who need a divine intervention and course redirection.

Please read through our healing experience and understand that we are working with the divine Law of As Above, So Below, As Within, So Without. When you have Soul in charge of structuring your life, governing your choices, protecting you, and acting as your parental authority figure, you do not need external leadership. If you surrender the ego to the authority of Soul, then suffering from the interference from outside authority figures is unnecessary. Test us. We know what we are sharing with you. It is our mission to move the One Human Body out of a lack of freedom of choice and into abundance, harmony, and balance for the greatest good and highest joy of all.

Healing Experience
Reclaiming Your Highest Vibrational Will

Visualize yourself pulling military boots and political banners with slogans out of your throat. Place the boots and banners in a big, bright-green kettle with boiling violet fire inside. Say, "I choose to surrender the will of the ego to the Will of Soul. I give any fear of speaking my Will to Source."

Place your hand on the crystal doorknob of the purple door. Open the door and step into the emerald meadow. Together with your divine inner child, divine feminine, and divine masculine, step into the gently flowing violet-fire river of transformation and forgiveness. Your divine inner child will reach up and touch your heart area. A door opens in your heart.

Say, "I call all of my parentless children out of me. I call all of my confused selves out of me. I call all of my rebels-without-a-cause selves and all of my people pleasers and integrity compromisers out of me. I call all of my enraged and powerless selves out of me. I call all of old-male and old-female thoughts and feelings out of me. And with gratitude and acknowledgment of your service to me, I release you into the violet-fire river, and I forgive you all, even if I don't know what I'm forgiving."

All leaderless selves flow out of you and into the violet-fire river. They float safely to the Central Sun on the horizon. Say, "I surrender the will of my ego to the Will of my Soul, one with the Central Sun."

The river will change into a brilliant cobalt blue with ribbons of magenta woven throughout. Say, "I call my divine feminine Will into my humanity so that I can feel my Truth, know my Truth, and follow my Truth." The magenta color will fill your throat and feel soothing.

Now say, "I call my divine masculine Will into my humanity so that I can voice my choices and know clearly what to do to live my highest vibrational life." The cobalt blue color fills your throat, and you say, "I matter to Creator!"

And then the cobalt and magenta river changes and becomes emerald and gold. The river rises above your head and becomes a giant energy snake of emerald and gold sparkles. Open your mouth and say, "Come to me, Will of my Heart. Tell me what I desire. Tell me where my Heart is leading me?" The energy instantly flows into your mouth and fills every atom of your humanity with the Heart Power of trust in Soul.

From this place of trust in the one authority who lives within you, we merge our energy with your energy. We send rainbow swords of undiluted love into the spines of every ego-centered leader on Schoolroom Earth, past, present, and future. We send their misused power of fear to the Central Sun. One Human Body, thank you for learning to surrender to the highest Will.

❖❖❖

Transforming the
Games of Warfare
and Military Action

Every human being has a defiant, energized, and resilient young masculine living within them that may or may not be expressing himself in a positive and productive way. This young masculine wants to be a hero helping others. At his highest vibration, he is the masculine aspect of your divine inner teenager. However, when he is frustrated and feeling powerless, he is the perfect prey for the old male who tells him to compete and win to have power and status in the world.

Schoolroom Earth's divine young masculine can be found anywhere there is innovation, positive change, respect for those different from oneself, motivation, honesty, and courage. On the other end of the vibration spectrum, the fearful young masculine reveals himself in the need to fight with himself or others, hide and self-destruct, or compete to survive no matter whom he may hurt in his climb upward. When he anticipates that he will not get his way or have his will acknowledged, he can turn violent and explode in pent-up rage. In this state, the old male comforts him and tells him that he can help him get what he wants and get it now.

When this fearful young masculine is being parented by the old male, he can give you "road rage" so that you drive your life too fast and too hard. If he is ignored or punished by his old male and female parents, he can manifest as ego-centeredness, addiction, and impulsive behaviors and be adamant that he needs a gun. The mindset of the fearful young masculine-old male and old female combination may even demonstrate the impetus to harm others either verbally or physically when he feels threatened.

Because the fearful young masculine, with the old male and female as his parents, lives within the One Human Body, he appears in the global reality as the person on the news who used a weapon to harm himself and others. Tragically, he lives within the decision-makers who instigate war games, biological and chemical war plans, and all militant action on Schoolroom Earth. This wounded teenager, expressing through egos with power, can be charismatic and convincing that his way is the only way. He lacks a sense of emotional security no matter how much confidence he might show. Underneath his armor is a frightened boy who knows something is very wrong with himself, and he often projects this onto others whom he wants to punish.

Let us work together to transform him and free him from the clutches of the old male and female. Once he is free within you, he will help us to free the young masculine from the right shoulder of the One Human Body.

To begin, ask within and see where your own young masculine has appeared in the movie of your life. Has his behavior changed as you have matured and committed to a spiritual journey? Are you able to validate when he is acting from a place of undiluted love with balanced energy that incorporates his feminine, Heart, and Soul? Acknowledging your young masculine when he is acting from his Heart Power changes your life for the better immediately. Because of the Law of One, your empowerment of your divine inner young masculine helps eliminate war, warfare, weapons, gangs, destructive drugs, and hostile military and police action.

We begin by transforming those areas where the heroic young masculine has given authority to the old male to be his judging father and the old female to be his critical mother.

Healing Experience
Working with the Young Masculine

Close your eyes and step into a white-fire vortex sprinkled with rainbow magic dust. Invite your divine inner child to join you. Ask your divine inner child if they know where the young masculine can be found within your vessel. Because we are transforming his lowest vibration look in your liver. You can feel your liver just below your ribcage on the right, and it is the organ where you store anger. If he is very angry, you may feel his fist raised in your gallbladder, located just above your liver in your solar plexus area.

Follow your divine inner child and when you find the young masculine, ask him if he is ready to release and forgive his frustrations and rage. If his answer is yes, ask him to transform into a violet-fire erupting volcano. Help him by seeing violet and scarlet lava explode out through the top of your head, sending the lava upward to the Central Sun.

Breathe deeply and ask him, "What do you need and what do you want in order to manifest our greatest good and highest joy?" Let him know that you truly care about his unmet needs and desires, and you want to work together to support his manifestation of freedom and success.

Offer him a cup filled with white-gold singing light and ask him to drink in the undiluted love of Mother-Father-God. Let him know you want him to feel safe, wanted and valued, and courageous.

After the lava has finished pouring out through the top of your head, and you feel cool and calm, go with him and your divine inner child into the cave of Mr. Grudge. Mr. Grudge symbolizes the resentment that your young masculine feels. He grows bigger when you are blind to the young masculine's feelings and restrict his freedom.

Mr. Grudge is made of gallstones, symbolic or real, and he looks like an unfriendly but not frightening monster. Say, "Out you go, Mr. Grudge who dines on my self-confidence and eats my self-worth for breakfast!" We will help you push Mr. Grudge into the violet-fire ocean of transformation and forgiveness. Take a moment to look around in the cave of Mr. Grudge. Let us help you clear out his arsenal of weapons of destruction. Please do not attach to any weapons you see in your solar plexus. All weapons are symbolic of fear. Clearing these symbols from you helps us to clear weapons from the global movie of Schoolroom Earth.

See the Central Sun fill your solar plexus with white-gold divine love until the energy is radiating from your every chakra and pore. Ask your young masculine to take you to his negative parents, the old king and the old queen whom he has given positions of authority.

Ask your young feminine teenager self to join the effort. She has been watching from the sidelines all along. She opens the floor underneath the old king and queen and releases all their victims (self-loathing thoughts and feelings of jealousy and betrayal). Say, "I release it all. I forgive it all. I choose to be free of my inner conflict and war with myself, NOW!

Your divine inner child pushes a button, and everything becomes a sea of violet, sapphire blue, turquoise, ruby, coral, emerald, and gold. Proclaim, "Love transforms fear into love."

Ask your young feminine teenager self to merge with your divine feminine, and ask your young masculine to now merge with your divine masculine. Feel the healing of your ego expand as you allow more Soul Power to support the ego than ever before.

Now enter your creativity garden and ask your divine Self to show you what has been newly planted that is sure to astound you. Be sure to write it down after you open your eyes so the idea is grounded.

We have another assignment for you. We need your help in transforming fear's old male and old female vibrations that permeate violent video games, aggressive sports, war games and military training, social media, news media, violent films and TV programs, pornography, corporate hierarchy, gangs, organized crime, and all other vibrationally similar thoughts, feelings, and experiences on Schoolroom Earth.

We will begin by doing some healing on the trapped young masculine held in the shoulder of the One Human Body. Once he is released, we will merge our energy with your energy and soak Schoolroom Earth and the astral filter with an all-loving, penetrating purple rain.

Healing Experience
Transforming or Eliminating Conflict from the Inside Out

Take a deep breath in and say, "I Am a cell of undiluted love, living within the One Human Body." See yourself glow like a fiery sunrise. Send the ruby, coral, and yellow of the fiery cell that is you into the cells surrounding you. We add our love to your love. We are all directing this healing into the right shoulder of the One Human Body.

The shoulder begins to glow and purge broken and angry boys, young men, and older men. They fall like shards of glass into the violet-fire lake where the One Human Body is swimming. Let us say, "I Am forgiving all betrayal by fear's old male and old female. I Am choosing to put the vibration of undiluted love in all I do, say, think, feel, and experience. I Am the One Human Body, divine child of Creator."

A violet-fire rain begins to fall over the entirety of Schoolroom Earth. It is made of undiluted love and because it is the highest vibrational energy, it fuses with the atoms of all that is, material and nonmaterial, living and nonliving, seen and unseen. Let us say, "Fear, we call you Home to Source. We thank you for your service to the One Human Body, and we say that your service is no longer needed."

Imagine that you take a photo of a gun and run the photo under purple water and then bright green water. See the photo change into a picture of a beautiful garden where the roses have no thorns.

Transforming the
Patriarchal Hierarchy

For fear to ensnare your ego and pull it away from Soul, it must accomplish two things. First, it must lower the vibration of your masculine logical-rational mind and create an illusionary wall of separation from the feminine emotional-intuitive mind. Second, fear's old male must then take charge of your male mind and dominate your thoughts and actions. When these two things happen, your suppressed logical mind will try to control your intuitive-creative mind (the twin sisters) until you no longer allow this hierarchy to live within you. When your mind is your own, grounded, gut intuition supported by good common sense will be the way that you solve problems and make choices. Having an open mind will organically make working for the oppressive old male who runs the "good old boys" club very distasteful. With this stated, we acknowledge that the patriarchal hierarchy is archaic and to change its well-established global structure may seem impossible—unless you invite in the vast wealth of the feminine.

For humanity to transform the inequality perpetuated for eons of time by the patriarchal hierarchy, the One Human Body must acknowledge and value the greater ability of the feminine mind and her access to Creator's knowledge. Those who use the feminine mind may be employed in service jobs that some see as less important because they are not high on the patriarchal male's achievement ladder. No one's service on Schoolroom Earth has less value than another's when the service is needed to live a better life. The nurse is just as valuable as the top surgeon, the garbage worker is as important as the head chef, and the office administrator is as necessary as the CEO.

You may say to us, "But 12 Archangels, while the services themselves may be of equal value, payment for many of them is anything but equal or fair." Our response is for you to ask yourself what a fair wage looks like for yourself and let go of basing the answer on what you have been taught. Once the true answer has been validated by your divine inner child, ask for the fair wage to come to you through receiving from the Divine Mother. Be sure to express gratitude for the earnings that flow to you. Thanking Source for your paycheck raises the vibration of the money you earn. It helps this money do more for you.

Currency, in any form, belongs to the old male and old female unless you remove it from their control. Remember, the thoughtform of money needs to stay in the black box that you continue to give to Source as an ongoing practice. The patriarchal hierarchy has no backbone when money is taken out of the old male and female's power game, so take the money that comes into your movie out of their game. Go straight to Source for all you need to live a good life and feel free. Think from your feminine creative-intuitive mind, farm your creativity garden, do the work that makes your divine inner child the happiest, and offer your service because it brings you great joy.

If you would like to test our wisdom and step into the water of freedom one toe at a time, you can help the One Human Body wake from its slumber. Your creativity garden is growing a sellable product that will provide for you as you share it. Begin this exchange now, even if you believe you need to work for a corporation or institution until you feel safe to leave it. We understand that human beings must experience actual resources, opportunities, and financial earnings finding their way to you from Source. Thank you for asking Source to give you the proof you need right now and keep asking.

And if your creative endeavors require you to hire others to work with you, you can choose to pay them the going wage or take a deep breath, listen to your Heart, and ask them what they need to be paid to live a good life. If you do not have the money to pay them, then ask the Divine Mother of the Great Universe to receive their pay into your business. When each human being chooses to practice respect, trust, and generosity, life on Earth changes for the better.

We are going to give you a symbol to use for transforming this ancient, old-male saturated structure. You cannot misuse the symbol because it signifies the Law of As Above, So Below, As Within, So Without.

Healing Experience
Deep Cleansing for the Old Male and Old Female

Draw a large circle on a blank piece of paper. Say, "This circle represents Divine Oneness and the Great Universe. The shape represents the feminine.

Within the circle draw a triangle with equal sides. The triangle in our healing exercise represents Heart Power. See the circle fill with ruby singing light. Say, "This ruby circle represents the Divine Mother of the Great Universe." See the triangle as a doorway with emerald and golden singing light pouring through the opening.

The point of the triangle represents the "as above" of Heaven, and the base of the triangle represents the "so below" of Earth. Say, "This triangle represents the divine Law of As Above, So Below, As Within, So Without."

Ask your divine inner child to take the triangle from the circle and place it inside of a square. The square represents the masculine. See the square light up in sapphire blue singing light and say, "This square represents the Divine Father of the Great Universe."

Your divine inner child turns the triangle upside down so that the point is now at the bottom and the base of the triangle is at the top. When the triangle is turned upside down, it represents the money at the top of the corporate structure flowing to all the workers. Source flows through unhindered. Say, "I Am willing to experience the miracle of all people feeling valued and respected for their contribution to the care of the One Human Body and planet Earth."

Give the circle, square, and triangle to us, the 12 Archangels, so we can convert the symbols into energy that is ruby, sapphire blue, and emerald with golden sparkles.

Our last step is for you to walk with us into this grand river of singing light. As we step into the healing colors we say, "I Am sending the old female out of the One Human Body. I Am calling respect for the divine feminine into every cell of the One Human Body."

Now say, "I Am sending the old male and his structure out of every cell of the One Human Body. I Am calling the divine masculine, in balance with the divine feminine, into the One Human Body."

Watch as the river of multiple colors changes into the violet-fire river of transformation and forgiveness. Say, "I give thanks to the patriarchal hierarchy for all it has taught humanity, and I give thanks that it is now transforming into Heart Power! See the violet-fire river change into Trust and Heart Power, emerald and gold singing light. Say, "I Am choosing respect and equality for all."

Transforming Pollution and the Exploitation of Natural Resources

Mother Earth is an impressive teacher for all students attending her schoolroom. She reflects the negative and fearful thoughts and emotions that the human collective wishes to avoid. When needed, she increases the magnitude of her lesson and repeats it until mastered. Let us help you understand what she wants humanity to learn. Fear's old male and female seduce the One Human Body into the stress of constant doing. Doing is masculine, and the masculine is seen as having far greater importance than the feminine in daily life. Earth is feminine, and she asks the collective to value and respect the sensitive and compassionate Mother.

Deep in the consciousness (fueled by the subconscious) of the One Human Body is the belief that the feminine and her ability to love and care have less value than the masculine and his drive for success and power. Humanity projects this inequality onto Mother Earth because she is the feminine that nurtures and the feminine that can be taken advantage of and used. The fear of natural resources running out drives humanity to ignore their true mother and stay blind to the devastation of the planet.

What can you, as part of the One Human Body, do to transform this destructive and shocking imbalance? You can begin by slowing down and becoming aware of your negative thoughts and emotions. Lift the vibration of your negativity with gratitude and observe how Gaia responds to the positive transformation of your inner pollution. Doing this helps more than you may realize. You can be sure that the old male has a different agenda!

Fear's old male will continue to preach that instant gratification is the correct way to live. He says focus on money: having it and spending it. He tells you to take what you can now because there may not be anything left tomorrow. Stay on the hamster wheel, keep chasing the money, and keep overdoing. Don't think about the impact of the vibration of your thoughts, feelings, and actions.

The Divine Mother offers a different way to live. Every moment, Archangel Gaia surrounds you with the highest vibrational love and Truth. She encourages you to slow down so you can hear your intuition. She wants you to use your creative genius. How does this help her?

Do you know that burning the fuel of Soul to manifest products and services that benefit all is mirrored in your world as clean energy? Besides solar power, Mother Earth has the secrets, and microbes, for miraculous recycling of trash into treasure. Your scientists have the knowledge needed to heal Gaia's physical body. They understand that they must be brave and patient physicians, capable of enduring the resistance of the patriarchal hierarchy. The Divine Mother of the Great Universe is vibrationally helping these scientists stay focused, and together they are paving the way forward for the rescue of Earth.

With this acknowledged, we are hopeful that soon the One Human Body will agree that healing Earth, even though it does not "turn a profit," is more crucial than making money through manufacturing fossil fuels and plastics. The potential for reclaiming your planet is real, and the best place to begin is within, by piercing through the deception of the old male and female. Believe it or not, to repair Mother Earth requires all in the One Human Body to take responsibility for their negative thoughts and feelings. Fearful thoughts and low-vibration emotions on the inside become pollution and depletion of resources in the environment.

To change the global movie of air, water, and land pollution, global warming, resource depletion, and destruction of Earth, human beings must regain respect for the Divine Mother. Once the energy of the divine feminine flows freely into the consciousness, subconsciousness, and actions of humanity, Mother Earth will have the highest vibrational energy she needs to heal. Her body will no longer need to serve as the mirror reflecting the ignored and rejected emotions (including guilt and shame) back to her students.

Earth and all that is happening within her, on her surface, and in her environment offers to humanity reflections of their unacknowledged emotions, thoughts, and vibrations. Air pollution reflects humanity's negative, fear-infused, toxic thoughts. Water pollution reflects humanity's illness-producing emotions of rage, guilt, shame, and blame. Land pollution reflects humanity's disrespect of the physical body and disconnection with Soul. Exploitation of the land, animals, minerals, vegetation, trees, and even the people reflect the rape—taking without asking or repairing the damage. The continued use of fossil fuels shows that the human collective is living in the past and using the low-vibration, fear-saturated belief paradigms of their ancestors to create their current realities. Using solar power and clean energy sources demonstrates the positive use of human creativity (Soul Power) and mirrors high vibrational thoughts and feelings (air and water) that are free of contamination from the old male and old female.

Archangel Gaia, one with the Divine Mother of the Great Universe, asks you and all visitors of Earth to feel your feelings and lift the vibration of your thoughts and emotions if you truly wish to help her. Stay aware that fear's old female reinforces the painful memory of any life event when you experienced the lack of mothering or not receiving what you wanted when you wanted to have it. Such memories pull down your vibration and whether you like it or not, your earthly self will balance the loss of energy by replacing what you have been deprived of having.

When the energy balancing is not partnered with letting go of resentment and forgiving what needs to be forgiven, you may do it in a lower vibrational way that is unhealthy, disrespectful, or self-punishing. The Law of Energy tells you that such reactions can pull you down even further. It is worth your effort to be aware of your feelings and to heal. When you make the choice to balance the loss in the highest vibrational way, you help all concerned (Law of One) and this includes Mother Earth. She loves you beyond your understanding, and she helps you to connect with what you feel by being a loving mother who reflects the weather of your repressed feelings and emotions with actual weather events. Her body is constantly showing humanity what they need to release and to forgive. Moving into a neutral emotional place where inner peace and balance are the norm helps Earth to regain her strength and vitality. We offer you a summary of her emotional reflections in the list below.

► **Weather Events That Express Humanity's Emotions**
  • **Tornados** absorb pent-up anger from the local community and then release it when they touch down.
  • **Hurricanes, tropical storms, nor'easters, and typhoons** clear the emotion of a much larger area and often for the entire world.
  • **Snowstorms** shower the world, even though they may not cover the globe, with purification. The snow cleans the air of negative thoughts and puts a chill on anger and rage.
  • **Forest fires** display rage and also create transformation and rebirth for the areas effected and for the entire world.
  • **Rain** helps all beings of Earth to feel their feelings and to release them. Rain showers are like watching a sad movie when you need to cry. Angels cry when it rains because we add tears of joy to help shift the vibration of sorrow.

- **Fog** says that there is confusion in the air. Seeing yourself wearing a hat made of violet fire will help lift the foggy thoughts out of your head and help you to hear your intuition again.
- **Flooding** represents the emotional outpouring of human feelings that have no outlet. All floods say, "Let go of the past and say no to the old female pulling you down into victim consciousness."
- **Droughts** caused by water shortage are Mother Earth's way of saying, "Feel your feelings and connect with Heart. Let Trust fill you up so that new and better life experiences can come into your movie."
- **Hailstorms** bring the message of WAKE UP and look at your choices and behaviors. Let go of what is not making you happy and let go of the past. Forgive the past so that your future can be abundant.
- **Global warming** is the blatant message that money is not equal in value to living on a pristine planet that happens to be your mother. Global warming says, "I Am Archangel Gaia and I've had enough of this nonsense. Say no to greed and fear, choose love, and care about your health and your children, both the ones of your body and of your mind. Respect and cherish your mother for I have always cared for you."

Whatever the weather pattern may be, respecting the messages helps the storms to soften and the droughts to end faster. Just as your human body is a messenger for the weather of your emotions, Mother Earth is a messenger for what the One Human Body is feeling. You help her most by feeling your feelings and saying no thank you to the old female's offer to make you a victim. Ask the Divine Mother of the Great Universe to receive all you need into your reality in a way that also respects Mother Earth. Respect the feminine, be your own best mother and caregiver, listen to your intuition, and enjoy your creativity garden. All these things help Archangel Gaia to rebalance and restore. And one more important gift that you can give yourself is to stop compromising the truth of your Heart for money. Let the funds you need find their way to you from Source and trust that this responsibility belongs to Soul. When you shut down your feelings so that you can survive working at a job you despise, you only feed the old male, his greed, and his destruction of Earth.

Thank you for doing our deepest healing exercise for transforming pollution and rebalancing Mother Earth!

Healing Experience
Rebalancing the Power of the Divine Feminine

Close your eyes and take a deep and relaxing breath. Release the tension in your body. Breathe in calmness. Walk through the purple door and step into the ruby lake with your divine inner child and divine feminine. Say, "I am thirsty for Divine Mother's undiluted love. Thank you for filling me with emotional security and physical safety."

When you are fully saturated and hydrated with the ruby energy of the divine feminine and Divine Mother of the Great Universe, say, "I release and I forgive any toxic emotions and belief paradigms in my body. I send these emotions and limiting beliefs to the Central Sun to transform." The toxic emotions and hurtful beliefs will look like black dragons leaving your body. Thank them as they exit.

The divine inner child swirls the ruby water, and emerald singing light with gold sparkles begins to flow upward like a spring. Soak in the divine nectar of Trust and say, "I choose to trust my divine feminine and respect my divine inner child. I know that doing so helps Mother Earth to rebalance. I release and I forgive any negative, old-male thoughts of not-enough-for-me greed and control, and I send them to Divine Oneness to be transformed into love."

The nature Angel of your body appears in the emerald and gold spring. The Angel swirls the water of the ruby lake and sapphire blue diamonds appear. Other colors begin to flow from the emerald spring, and the healing fountain is growing tall and bright.

Take the cup offered to you from your nature Angel and drink in the love and respect for your body and for planet Earth. Say, "I acknowledge with vast gratitude my mother, Mother Earth. I choose to love her for all she gives to me. I thank her for providing me with my body. I thank my body for bringing into my awareness any emotions, feelings, and negative thought patterns that I might try to ignore."

Once you feel renewed, say, "I choose to allow the Divine Mother of the Great Universe to restore my feminine and through my atoms, molecules, and cells to restore the feminine of the One Human Body. I allow and I embrace."

Merge with your divine inner child and divine feminine and grow to the size of a great Angel. Hold planet Earth in your loving hands and bring her close to your Heart. Send her healing Heart Power and say, "Thank you, Earth. I love you and I am truly grateful for all you give to the One Human Body."

Stay in this sacred space until you feel ready to be your divine human self. Step out of the ruby lake and cross through the purple door. What kindness and mothering are you willing to offer yourself? To Mother Earth's inhabitants? To Mother Earth's body?

We thank you for your love of Archangel Gaia and of Divine Oneness.

Transforming Fear into Love

We are the 12 Archangels of the Central Sun, one with Divine Oneness and one with you, divine human being. We thank you for your willingness to transform fear into love and receive all you need from Source. We thank you for working with the divine laws that govern your schoolroom. We thank you for honoring your decision to come to Earth, to learn, to grow, and to discover your divinity in the intensity of your human experiences. We thank you for being aware of fear's old male and old female for they pull you away from abundance, health, and joy. We thank you for receiving, and we thank you for asking for all you wish to receive. Receiving from the Divine Mother restores the feminine of the One Human Body, and she desperately needs to be restored.

Ask. Trust. Receive. Give thanks. And always value the treasure of the genius ideas manifesting in your creativity garden. We invite you to say our mantra for you: "Fear out, love in. Lack out, wealth in. Suffering out, joy in. I am willing to surrender the will of the ego to the highest Will of Soul!"

To increase Heaven's freedom, undiluted love, and happiness, let your divine inner child heal your broken heart and leap into the unknown of ascending out of fear and into Heaven. It is your Soul's birthright to lack nothing. It is impossible for you to experience scarcity when your vibration stays at the frequency of undiluted love, the singing light of the Central Sun. Doing so as much as possible helps your Mother Earth to heal herself in surprising and miraculous ways.

Healing Experience
Healing the Divine Inner Child

Close your eyes and place your hands on your heart. Say, "Divine inner child, please raise my vibration to your vibration. Place your loving hands on my heart."

See little hands of singing rainbow light on your heart and say, "I love you my divine inner child. Thank you for helping me to grow more trusting and aware of your presence in this hour."

Do you feel your Heart Power flowing and meeting the love of Creator? We invite you to say together with your divine inner child, "Thank you, Soul, one with the Central Sun, for receiving a new and joyful childhood into my life. I allow my new childhood to be rich with freedom and one in which I feel safe, wanted, valued, and loved."

PART 7

Healing Experiences to Support Restful Sleep and Happy Receiving

A good sleep helps your ego grow younger, and a youthful attitude helps your ego connect with your divine inner child. Being together builds trust that all things are possible!

THE 12 ARCHANGELS OF THE CENTRAL SUN

To support your healing and its integration with your divinity, we invite you to enjoy our magical elixir (healing experiences) to support restful sleep. Fear's old male enjoys tormenting your mind with complaints, worries, and doubts at bedtime. All this anxiety can make it challenging for you to experience the peaceful and nourishing sleep that you need. The old female knows that exhaustion distracts you from remembering to use your spiritual tools to bring to you all that you need to feel loved and supported. We suggest that you choose one healing experience each night and surrender completely to it. The more you do the healing, the faster your sleep—and waking life—will improve. Enjoy!

Healing Experience
Goodbye Negativity and Good Night!

Close your eyes and see yourself jump into a white-gold energy swimming pool. Ask your guardian Angels to turn you into a sponge. Your Angels will gently squeeze out all that does not belong to you. Take a deep breath and say, "Goodbye negativity! I release all the fear that I have absorbed from my environment and send it to the Central Sun."

Again see yourself jump into the swimming pool and turn into a sponge. And again, ask the Angels to squeeze out the negativity. Do this until you feel squeaky clean. Once you sparkle, leave the swimming pool and step into a ruby shower with ruby love of the Divine Mother flowing over you.

Reach into your head and find the radio playing the news of the day along with all your worries about the past and future. The radio flips from station to station, one station plays a song while another reports what is wrong with the world and in your adult life. Take the radio out of your head and place it on the drain in the ruby shower of divine love.

Step away from the drain and say, "Goodbye negativity radio. Goodbye old male thoughts and old female feelings." Watch the radio completely dissolve in ruby energy and disappear down the drain.

Grab the super-soft ruby towel and wrap yourself in it. The towel transforms into your favorite ruby and gold pajamas. There is a translucent violet-fire river of transforming love flowing over, under, and through your bed. Climb into your emerald sheets, pull the turquoise comforter up to your chin and say, "I forgive the past. I surrender to a happier tomorrow." Reach over and gently kiss your divine inner child who is sleeping soundly next to you.

Sweet dreams, beloved child of Divine Oneness.

Healing Experience
Dragon's Roost with the Divine Inner Child

Close your eyes, take a deep breath, and step through the purple door. Your divine inner child is waiting for you, along with your dragon. You can be sure that this dragon is funny and colorful and has scales and dragon skin that are soft as velvet.

Before you climb onto the back of the dragon, please introduce yourself and ask your dragon its name. The dragon sends it to you telepathically. Once the introductions have been made, please take a seat behind your divine inner child on the back of the dragon.

Your divine inner child wraps its arms around the dragon's neck in a big hug and whispers, "Let's go home." And with a most elegant lift off, you are in the air heading to Soul's favorite star system.

Once on your home planet, your dragon will take you to their roost that resembles a magnificent palace that floats in midair. It is nighttime and the stars are twinkling.

Enjoy a tour of the palace, have a snack and beverage. Your divine inner child will take you to where you will sleep. Rainbow pajamas that smell like fresh-baked cookies are laid out carefully on the oh-so-comfortable bed dressed in turquoise linens, the color of dreams come true. Your bed has magic pillows that will sing you and your divine inner child to sleep.

Climb into bed and think about all you are grateful for in your life. Reflect on all you are learning that is helping you to receive. Kiss your divine inner child goodnight and off to sleep you go.

Sweet dreams, beloved child of the Great Universe.

Healing Experience
Divine Mothers' Palace of Renewal

Close your eyes and take some deep breaths until you feel calm and centered. Look for the purple door and notice that above the transom is a garland of roses in every shade of pink, red, and orange.

Open the door and cross the threshold and enter the Palace of the Divine Mothers. Your own divine feminine greets you, and she is holding the hand of your divine inner child.

Do you have a special divine mother that speaks to your Heart? All the Goddesses of Heaven are here: Mother Mary, Quan Yin, Rachel, Mary Magdalene, Hathor, Lakshmi, Radha, and many more. If you have beloved grandmothers or other loving wise women living in Heaven, they are also here waiting for you in the Divine Mothers' Palace of Renewal.

The Mothers take you and your divine inner child into their home. To the left is a ruby bath waiting to dissolve your troubles away. Soak in the bath and soak up the restoring and deeply healing energy of the Divine Mother. Drink from the gold goblet filled with ruby deliciousness that will refresh you and then make you very sleepy.

And just before you nod off, the Mothers transform the ruby bath into the most comfortable bed that you have ever experienced. The sensation of safety and security is lovely as is the soft scent of lavender mixed with the scents of your favorite flowers.

Lean over and kiss your divine inner child goodnight. Your divine inner child is already fast asleep and waiting to meet you in a wonderful dream.

Fill with gratitude for these heavenly Mothers who will work through the night to make sure that you feel like a new you in the morning.

Sweet dreams cherished child of the Divine Mother of the Great Universe.

Surfing with the 12 Archangels

Close your eyes and smile. Straight ahead is a white-gold archway made of singing light and through the opening you can see ocean-sized waves made of rainbows.

Step through the archway and look down at your feet. You are standing on a turquoise surfboard made of singing light, and this surfboard won't let you fall. In the distance you can see us riding the big rainbow waves with your divine inner teenager, and we are having an awesome time together!

Choose a wave and do a turtle roll (turn upside down in the wave). Say, "I surrender to my biggest dreams come true." When you come out of the wave know that your prayer is being answered because your divine inner teenager has already sent your dream to Mother-Father-God.

And now it is your turn to do something wonderful with us. We ask your Soul to merge with you and become a giant Angelic being made of undiluted love. We toss you Schoolroom Earth, like a volleyball. Take the ball and dip your school into a rainbow wave. Once she is saturated, place Earth on the end of your surfboard and watch your school fill up with turquoise singing light. Say, "Schoolroom Earth, thank you for filling up with the energy of love and freedom." Give the Earth a hug and gently toss her back to us.

The rainbow waves transform into smooth, soft clouds that take the shape of a comfortable bed. Your turquoise surfboard flips you onto your bed, next to your divine inner teenager. The surfboard transforms into a light-as-air turquoise comforter. Lean over and kiss your divine inner teenager goodnight.

And we bring out the stars in the night sky with a mix of shimmering northern lights.

Sweet dreams fellow traveler and surfer of the Great Universe. We keep you safe and embraced in undiluted love.

Healing Experience
Merlin's Cabin and Cocoa

Close your eyes and say, "Merlin's cabin." Step through the purple door and enter a scene where the ground is covered in snow and the flowers are in full bloom. The trees have ripe fruit on their branches and the air is warm and clear. You are wearing your favorite sandals and summer attire. Merlin's world knows no such thing as cold, only forever beauty and grace.

There is a path made of gemstones that circles around a pond and heads to a cabin where purple smoke and silver stars rise from the chimney. Your divine inner child is waiting for you inside the cabin. No need to knock at the door; Merlin is expecting you. He is styling his favorite brightly colored Hawaiian shorts, and he has a purple hat made just for you.

Take a seat at the kitchen table and place your purple wizard's hat on your head. Your hat matches that of your divine inner child's. Merlin offers you a cup of steaming cocoa that is made of undiluted love. Do not worry about the purity of the ingredients because the only ingredients are love and peace.

Drink your cocoa with special happy-dream magic stirred into the beverage. Merlin asks you to tell him what you desire to experience more of in earthly life and once he has your answer, he vanishes into his laboratory.

Merlin returns with an emerald watering can and proceeds to water your head with violet-fire rain drops. He says to you, "Let go of all the guilt and sorrow in your mind and body." All you need to do is to say, "I allow all the guilt and sorrow in my vessel to be transformed into love."

You are now a beautiful shade of violet and ready for a deepest healing sleep. Climb the spiral stairs to the bedroom of your divine inner child. The bed is extravagant, with purple, ruby, and emerald linens. Everything smells wonderfully clean and fresh.

As you turn down the covers, pajamas magically appear on your body, and they match those of your divine inner child. Merlin gives you a sleeping potion made of undiluted love and the stuff that happiest dreams are made of. It tastes delicious.

Lean over and kiss your divine inner child goodnight. Merlin and your Helpers in Heaven are working on delivering that which will bring you joy in your earthly life. It will arrive in your movie very soon.

Merlin turns off the light and the stars appear overhead.

Sweet dreams beloved one. All is well.

Healing Experience
Into the Purple Sea

Take a deep breath in and exhale slowly, releasing the tension of the day from your body. Close your eyes and step through the purple door. Straight ahead is Archangel Michael's car wash, only it is for humans without their cars. Your divine inner child is waiting for you at the entrance.

Sit down in the ruby recliner next to your divine inner child. There are more ruby recliners that appear behind you and any hurting selves, of any age, take these seats.

The chairs move on a solar powered track into the car wash, and everything becomes a brilliant electric blue. Brushes made of Light and Sound come down from above and through the back of your recliner. Violet-fire suds shower you and everything looks as hilarious as it sounds.

The car wash is cleaning you of any negative thoughts and emotions that you may have absorbed from your environment. It is also vacuuming the old male and old female out of your human vessel and freshening your being with truth, honesty, and integrity.

Out of the car wash comes your ruby recliner, and it transforms into a ruby boat. Your divine inner child is sitting next to you. The car wash has become a violet-fire sea where the dolphins and whales are Angel physicians of superior training. All your hurting selves are now transformed with undiluted love and have integrated with you. This occurred when the warm golden-sun blowers dried you off just before the car wash exit.

Your ruby boat is swept into the undertow of the violet-fire sea, and you are caught in a gold net and taken by the dolphins into a castle made of living coral. So that you won't be frightened, the whales have changed themselves into Angels, and they welcome you to lie down on a ruby sofa with plush pillows.

You are going to have a DNA scrub of all that you no longer need to carry around in your cells, mind, or Heart. Say, "I release it all. I forgive it all."

Lean over and kiss your divine inner child because you are going to sleep now. When you wake up, you will feel so much better and clearer than before.

Sweet dreams, brave transformer. We thank you for being a cell in the One Human Body, and through you, we help all. We protect you from all sides, and everything is getting better for all concerned.

Healing Experience
Emerald and Ruby in a Golden Nest Egg

Close your eyes and say, "I surrender to the loving care of Soul." Repeat until you feel peaceful and safe.

Step through the purple door and into your creativity garden. Your divine inner child, divine inner teenager, divine feminine, and divine masculine are waiting for you. Your divine inner child takes you by the hand and leads you through a hidden garden gate to your right.

You step into a field where huge golden eggs are growing as if they were giant pumpkins. One of the eggs has opened down the middle and has emerald singing light radiating from the inside.

Reach into the emerald center of the egg and say, "I allow myself to be surprised by a miracle of joy when I wake up in the morning." Look at the ruby stone that is now in your hand. Place the stone under your tongue and let it dissolve. As it dissolves, it fills you with the security that you are significant to God. You are seen, heard, and valued by Creator.

Your divine feminine, divine masculine, divine inner teenager, and your divine inner child circle the golden egg and begin to hum softly. The egg transforms into a golden bed with ruby linens, and it looks so inviting that you climb right in and snuggle under the covers.

Lean over and kiss your divine inner child. Your divine inner child leans over and kisses your divine inner teenager who then leans over and kisses your divine feminine, who leans over and kisses your divine masculine.

Dreaming together with Soul has never felt so safe and wonderful.

Sweet dreams precious being of Divine Oneness. We are protecting all your golden eggs!

Healing Experience
Mother Earth's Haven

Close your eyes and take a relaxing breath. Step into the purple door disguised as a tunnel lit with emerald lights. A gentle violet-fire rain is falling on your head.

The tunnel opens into a forest filled with giant trees, grander in height and stature than the giant redwood forest. The mother tree calls to you telepathically, and she says, "Time to come home, dear children." You notice that your divine inner child is holding your hand and somehow you are the same age.

The mother tree's roots are huge, and in the middle of them, right in front of you, they form into a large house. The door is open, and you can smell wonderful things cooking on a stove.

Mother Earth serves you your favorite home-cooked meal and not to worry, no animals or plants were harmed to make your dinner. Mother Earth uses the energy of the Central Sun to create the meals on her menu, just like meals were made a long, long time ago.

Your eyes are drawn to the high roof of her house, and you notice magnificent butterflies resting on the upper beams. A honeycomb sits lower down, and honey from it drips into a large pot. The queen bee peaks her head out and greets you warmly.

A baby black bear, larger than you and your divine inner child, saunters over and rolls on her back so you can rub her belly. As you do so, answers to problems are resolved instantly in your mind.

After you visit with the other children of Mother Earth, she asks you to lie down on a soft bed covered in rabbit fur, silk, and butterfly wings. Remember, no animals or plants have been harmed to create your bed. Your bed is made of the energy of the Central Sun as it was done long, long ago.

And as you rest on the bed, Mother Earth rubs your feet, and you feel very relaxed and incredibly safe and loved. Your divine inner child is already fast asleep.

Lean over and kiss your divine inner child goodnight. Mother Earth will be working on you through the night and through you, she will be touching and healing the One Human Body too.

Let the healing soak in and receive it for it is given with total undiluted love.

Sweet dreams, child of Earth, child of love, Child of Creator.

Healing Experience
Gratitude for You

Close your eyes, stand under a violet-fire waterfall of cleansing energy, and breathe in innocent pink love. Send the pink love to your divine inner child and say, "You are innocent. I am innocent, and I am worthy of receiving all I need from the Great Universe." Repeat until you feel the old female leave your vessel. Make sure she takes her baggage and cooking gear with her.

Once you feel light and free, step through the purple door into the emerald meadow of Heart. Look for the giant pink lotus bloom floating on a ruby pond. The lotus has a lovely bed right in the middle of it.

Step into the ruby pond, holding the hand of your divine inner child, and say, "I am grateful for me. I am grateful for my humanity. I am grateful for my divinity. I am eternally grateful."

Wade out to the lotus blossom and touch one of the pink petals. It turns into a guardian Angel who lifts you and your divine inner child onto the bed, complete with pink pillows and a rainbow energy duvet.

Your guardian Angel opens a book and begins to read to you all the wonderful things that Divine Oneness appreciates in you. With each phrase of praise you hear, say, "Yes, I acknowledge that this is true, and I am grateful for me."

When the Angel has finished reading the list, we ask that you say, "I am willing to experience the miracle of the One Human Body waking up to their innocence and worthiness."

As you climb into bed on the floating blossom, we say to you that each petal is another Angel, and all Angels hold you in their love and gratitude.

Lean over and kiss your divine inner child and say, "Sweet dreams, priceless gem of Soul."

Enjoy your sleep and know that every cell, thought, and feeling is being filled with new awareness of your value to Creator. YOU MATTER TO GOD.

Healing Experience
Emerald Forest

Close your eyes and walk through the purple door. In the emerald meadow, your dragon and divine inner child wait for you.

Your dragon begins to drum a beat with its tail. A stairway appears that goes down into the ground. Your divine inner child throws gold and white sparkles onto the stairway, and it reverses and goes up into the sky, through the center of a bright green wreath decorated in beautiful colors and ornaments.

Follow your dragon and divine inner child up the stairs and through the grand wreath. Say, "I do believe in Fairy Angels. I do believe in Fairy Angels."

And you walk into a vast world of tall trees and observe beauty like you have never seen before. You are high in a treehouse that has no roof but is decorated with twinkling lights that move and dance around the room. The wind is like a violin's bow, and the leaves are its strings. The birds are different in this serene realm, and their songs play in harmony with the wind. What you may not see until your eyes adjust is the community of Fairy Angels also playing musical instruments and singing with their thoughts!

You and your divine inner child are dressed in shades of green that match the foliage. You are both covered in bells that tinkle gently and mix perfectly with the orchestra of wind, leaves, singing thoughts, and flute-like birds. Give your delicate human self a moment to completely submerge into this heavenly environment where fear has no place. You are very welcomed here and expected!

An ageless woman with long jade and golden hair, dressed in greens and reds, appears and offers you a delicious drink that is not liquid but made of swirling colors. She is very lovely, and she speaks telepathically in a way that sounds like melodious music. Her magical voice melts any ego defensiveness or resistance like hot toast melts butter.

She is the Fairy Goddess Illumina, and she welcomes you and your divine inner child to rest in her home in the forest for as long as you like. She lets you know that while you sleep, the fairies will do energy work on your ego to make it easier for you to create and to receive.

She points to where you will be sleeping, but there is nothing there. Your divine inner child seems to be sleeping in midair, and so Illumina smiles and picks you up and places you next to your divine inner child. Lean over and kiss your divine inner child who is now singing along with the fairies. Focus on the subtle sounds awakening forgotten parts of you and enjoy magical dreams filled with good news.

When you wake up, you will be in your own bed at home. Visiting the Fairy Angels does far more than you may know. Give yourself time to integrate and do visit your creativity garden today. Fairies can make anything grow.

We wish you a glorious day with a surprise that delights you and makes you truly happy.

Healing Experience
Orchard of Ever-Growing Currency Trees

Close your eyes, take a deep breath in, and walk through the purple door. Your divine feminine is sitting behind the wheel of a bright magenta convertible and the top is down. Sit in the passenger seat and wave to your divine inner child and divine inner teenager who are sitting together in the back seat.

Your divine feminine drives through the emerald meadow, past your creativity garden, and into an orchard with many trees. These trees are like nothing you could ever imagine because their leaves are made of gold and imprinted on them are the words, "Pick me. Spend me. Share me." They produce two new leaves for each leaf picked.

Your divine feminine opens the trunk and there is a basket for each of you. Before you begin to pick the leaves that will manifest in your life as that which you desire most, there is something that you must do: Give thanks that the energy that you are made of has more value and is more impressive than all the money on Earth. Acknowledge this and feel it deep within your marrow. Take your basket and enjoy picking some leaves and watching them regrow instantly and double in number.

After harvesting the currency trees, your divine feminine starts a violet-fire bonfire inside a sapphire blue ring of flame. All of you toss your leaves into the fire and say, "I let go of any fear of not having enough. I am willing to experience the miracle of remembering that all I need and all I desire will be given to me by Soul and Creator in perfect divine timing, obeying the divine laws."

Your divine feminine and divine inner teenager return to the car and find a small tent made of silk. When the tent is pitched, it transforms into the home of the Ascended Masters who have come to give you guidance. The Teachers who are assigned to help you are already inside the tent waiting for you. Lie down on the comfortable mattress covered in bright colors. Listen, for they will tell you all you want to know about your earthly life. They will explain how your experiences teach you to value yourself and Divine Oneness.

Don't worry about the gold leaves. They will cross the veil from Heaven to Earth and materialize as Soul's desire for your humanity. This you cannot block, even if receiving is still something new and perhaps a bit scary for you.

Lean over and kiss the twin sisters of intuition and creativity and enjoy a mystical nap where all your questions are answered.

Sweet dreams in comfort and Trust, most wise child of the Great Universe.

Healing Experience
Golden Pyramid of Initiation with the 12 Archangels

Close your eyes and take a deep breath in and exhale slowly and completely. Say, "I surrender to the joy of my Soul."

Turn the crystal doorknob on the purple door and step into the emerald meadow. In a garden filled with springtime flowers, there is a pyramid of gold-white singing light. You can see that your divine inner child is inside, and you can see tall figures standing near. There is no entrance; however, there is a way in.

Say, "Divine inner child of Heart, please let me be with you and the Angels."

And you are now inside a large room that is bare, except for the lanterns emitting soothing gold-white loving light. Lie down on what looks like a white marble table. Say, "I surrender to the unconditional love and compassion of Creator." As you state your intention to surrender, the marble table begins to feel different, no longer cool and masculine but feminine, soft, and gentle.

The bed of eternal life reforms to support your body in total comfort. Your bed is now ruby, your pillow is emerald, and your coverlet is opalescent. The pyramid is lightly scented with jasmine, neroli, lavender, and rose.

We have invited you here to our sacred space to help move your residual scarcity beliefs out of you. We need you to be willing to let go of the lies you have been taught. We can only tell the Truth because we are made of Truth, and truthfully, poverty is a lie that only works if you live in the illusion of fear. We offer you the choice for love, and we invite you to receive your abundance.

Your divine inner child is standing next to you, and they kiss you lightly on your forehead. You are going into Angel surgery now; it is painless and will set you free.

As you drift off to sleep, please say, "I matter to Creator. I surrender the not enough of the ego and ask for all lack to be transformed into true wealth for me and for the One Human Body. I thank you, Angels, that Schoolroom Earth benefits from my surrender. I choose LOVE!"

Sweet dreams beloved one.

We thank you for using your abundance wisely and for staying connected to Heart. If doubt enters, ask to be filled with the golden nectar you love to drink. Yes, Divine Child, receive in Trust and let it refill your Heart Power. Heart and Soul will keep your life moving forward because the Divine Mother will make sure of it!

LOVE ETERNAL
THE 12 ARCHANGELS OF THE CENTRAL SUN

Acknowledgments

With every atom of my humanity, I thank the 12 Archangels of the Central Sun for sharing their incredible love and wisdom through me.

Gratitude beyond this world for the support of my husband, Michael Wolk. I think he must be an Angel on Earth.

I would like to acknowledge the fine talent, steadfastness, and patience of Jane Lahr, Eileen Duhné, and Stephanie Allen.

I am grateful to Regina Meredith for her friendship and willingness to help the 12 Archangels with their mission of helping humanity. Thank you, Christiane Northrup, Michael Sandler, and Alex Ferrari for your faith in the Angels and for sharing their channeled wisdom with your audiences.

I am beyond grateful to the courageous students who have taken the Angels' advanced training. Thank you for being my teachers and for your service to Schoolroom Earth.

Always, I am grateful for my friends who are my family and my family that truly are beautiful friends.

Thank you to the owners and talented staff of Inner Traditions for publishing this book as well as its predecessor, *Lessons from the 12 Archangels*.

The 12 Archangels' Glossary of Terms

12 Archangels. A team of Angelic healers who can expand their loving touch anywhere throughout the Great Universe. An infinite number of all-Powerful beings of Light and Sound who help humanity and Earth to rise from the vibration of fear and return to the vibration of love.

abundance. The excess of blessings received when a human being transforms their fears and asks the Great Universe for what they need and want. Creator's response to prayers. Positive results from holding the highest vibrational intention to receive from Soul and Source. *See also* prosperity; wealth.

alchemical. The property of undiluted (divine) love that changes fear into love.

Angel. A being made of undiluted love helping you to forgive the past and open further to receive from the Great Universe.

Archangel Gabriel. All-loving force of clear communication flowing from Creator. Gabriel's energy is pastel blue or aqua. Think of fresh air.

Archangel Gaia. All-loving energy that embodies Mother Earth. Gaia is the mother of all human beings and Creation on Earth. *See also* Gaia.

Archangel Metatron. All-loving force of the highest vibrational gratitude and success that comes with happiness and freedom. The Angel's energy is turquoise singing light, the combination of the Will and heart chakras.

Archangel Michael. All-loving force of highest Will, courage, and Truth at the vibration of undiluted love. Michael's energy is the sapphire blue singing light of the Will chakra.

Archangel Victoria. All-loving force of divine justice, victory, and balance. Sister to Archangel Michael. Victoria's energy is the white-fire singing light of purification, the eighth chakra.

astral filter. The protective vibrational space between Heaven and Earth where fear and negativity are absorbed. The astral filter is the same as the astral super sponge. The subconscious works like the astral filter, holding the vibrational space between the past and the present, and the wounded ego and the Heart.

Central Sun. God's energy that is both Sound and Light at the vibration of undiluted love. The Source where all Souls come from and vibrational destination for all Souls studying on Schoolroom Earth. *See also* Creator; chakra; Divine Oneness; Great Universe; singing light.

chakra. A battery of Creator's energy used for healing and the evolution of consciousness. Chakras come in an infinite array of colors; however, most humans see them as the primary colors of God's rainbow. *See also* singing light.

coral singing light. The energy of the Soul (second) chakra. Coral singing light helps release sexual abuse and facilitate the balance of the masculine and feminine. It is also a wonderful energy to fire up one's creativity.

creative imagination. The brain function that the feminine intuitive brain uses to visualize the steps outlined in a healing experience. The creative imagination operates best at the vibration of love and joy.

creativity. The expression of Soul's genius in ways that obey the divine laws and support receiving wealth from Source. *See also* wealth.

creativity garden. The space within the feminine-intuitive and creative brain where genius ideas are planted by Soul. *See also* Heart; Heaven.

Creator. The undiluted and creative love energy of Mother-Father-God. Divine Oneness lives within the Creator. *See also* Central Sun; Great Universe.

deep subconscious. The storage caverns, molecules, and atoms capable of holding the pain and suffering from past lives and ancestry. Clearing the deep subconscious of fear greatly benefits receiving from Source.

divine feminine of Soul. The feminine of your higher Self, the divine mother of your ego and inner child. She is the receptive and grounding aspect of Soul.

divine inner child. The messenger for Soul and doorway to Heaven and the pipeline for receiving abundance. The divine inner child is the pure loving and innocent aspect of your inner child.

divine inner teenager. This is the divine inner child aged twelve to twenty. The divine inner teenager gives motivation for implementing creative genius ideas. This aspect of Soul is courageous and unstoppable.

divine masculine of Soul. The masculine of your higher Self, the divine father of your ego and inner child. He is the manifesting and protective aspect of Soul.

Divine Oneness. Synonymous with Creator, all sentient beings in the Great Universe are part of Divine Oneness. *See also* Central Sun; Great Universe.

divine Self. The divine Self is the divine inner child, divine feminine, and divine masculine united. *See also* Soul.

DNA scrub. The action of undiluted love energy removing the vibration of fear from DNA and RNA molecules. Although called a "DNA scrub," the cleansing reaches to the quantum level (subatomic particles of energy).

dragon. Creator's expression of emotional energy that at the vibration of Heaven is all loving, magical, and protective. At the vibration of fear, dragons symbolize emotions of rage that need to be released through breathing out through the top of the head. Dragons can be of any color, size, and shape.

ego. The individuation and expression of a Soul experiencing Schoolroom Earth. The ego can experience fear and fall prey to fear's archetypes of the old male and old female. The ego can believe in separation from Divine Oneness where Soul knows this is impossible. The ego can fracture into multiple selves of different ages.

emerald singing light. The energy of the heart chakra. Visualizing emerald helps the ego to enter the creativity garden of Heart.

emerald with golden sparkles. The energies of the heart and solar plexus chakras fused together to facilitate raising the vibration of the masculine mind. Emerald with golden sparkles is the color of Creator's Trust energy and Heart Power.

empath. A being who senses, feels, and often responds to the emotions of other beings. Empathic beings also absorb negative (less than happy) vibrations of emotions from others and from the environment.

Fairy. An Angelic being responsible for facilitating miracles. Angels that bring awakening, fun, and growth.

Fairy Goddess Illumina. A Divine Mother of the fairies and an energy healer with great Power. *See also* Heart Power.

Father of the Great Universe. Thought, or light, at the vibration of undiluted love in action. The highest vibrational doing, giving, and manifesting into form. The Divine Father's energy gives courage, clarity, and motivation.

fear. Anything less in vibration or frequency than undiluted love. Fear creates the illusion of separation between particles and beings of Creator's energy. *See also* fear's old male and fear's old female.

fear's old female. Lower vibrational feelings such as guilt, shame, unworthiness, and resentment. Lower vibrational emotions such as anger, self-loathing, unresolved grief, or punishment.

fear's old male. Lower vibrational ego thoughts that are critical, judging, condescending, limiting, and controlling. The old male seduces the ego into believing that you are not enough and unworthy of asking and receiving from Source.

feminine brain. The larger part of your mind that is intuitive, creative, visionary, and receptive. Both the Heart and creativity garden live within the feminine brain. *See also* divine feminine of Soul.

fuchsia singing light. The energy of the third-eye chakra when used to expand the creative imagination or inner sight.

Gaia. The Archangel that embodies Mother Earth. Gaia is the home of Schoolroom Earth. *See also* Archangel Gaia.

genius. An idea, inspiration, or solution originating from Soul and Heaven's Helpers. The idea or solution will make perfect common sense and comes with a feeling of clarity, hope, or happiness.

golden or yellow singing light. The energy of the solar plexus chakra. Golden or yellow singing light brings in self-esteem, happiness, confidence, and personal power.

golden sparkles. Sparks of Mother-Father-God's undiluted love that increase the healing power and joy of any singing light.

Great Universe. All that exists in form or not in form. The Great Universe is held together with undiluted love. *See also* Central Sun; Creator; Divine Oneness.

guardian Angel librarian. The Angel that protects all your beliefs and memories, conscious and subconscious. This Angel may be the guardian Angel that travels with your Soul during lives on Earth and beyond.

guardian Angels. The Angelic beings that escort you to Schoolroom Earth and love and protect you while in school. Guardian Angels can grow in number (if needed). They remain consistent throughout a Soul's incarnations anywhere in the Great Universe.

healer. A being who facilitates the shift in vibration from lower to higher. Healers exist on Earth and throughout the Great Universe. Angels are healers as are trees, pets, and children. Any person can act as a healer, whether conscious of the act or unaware.

healing experience. Highest vibration visualization exercise that works by slowly and consciously reading through it. By holding the intention that the experience is wonderful, the healing can go even deeper.

Heart. The sanctuary in the feminine intuitive brain that exists at the vibration of undiluted love or Heaven. The purple door opens to the Heart where the garden of creativity resides.

Heart Power. The highest vibrational energy of attraction that brings exactly what is needed for success. Heart Power comes from the divine inner child as well as Creator.

Heaven. The energetic space and vibration of undiluted love. The Heart sanctuary where Souls gather to commune and grow.

Heaven's Helpers. Angels, Ascended Masters, loved ones who have passed, and wise Souls in Heaven who offer support and wisdom to human beings learning lessons on Earth.

Helpers in Heaven. Your personal team of Angels and Guides.

humanity. All Souls attending Schoolroom Earth who have created egos of any vibration at any moment, past, present, and future.

intuition. Guidance flowing from Soul through the feminine brain.

karma. Lessons that need to be learned on Schoolroom Earth. *See also* karmic homework.

karmic homework. The agreements that your Soul made to support your ego in transforming fear into love during this life. Each new life accepts the unfinished karma of all past lives.

lack. Having less than what is needed or wanted. Lack consciousness is a way of thinking where the fear of scarcity or less than enough overshadows one's choices.

Law of As Above, So Below, As Within, So Without. The vibration of undiluted love in Heaven above that can be found on Earth below.

When there is love within, the love manifests without as all things beneficial.

Law of Energy. Divine Oneness is energy, and all energy is undiluted love. On Earth, energy can drop in vibration due to fear. Lift the vibration of energy with gratitude, forgiveness, compassion, and unconditional love.

Law of One. All particles of Creator's energy live within the Great Universe and sense each other. Separation between particles is an illusion. When one particle of energy or one being helps another, all particles and all beings benefit from the help.

library of beliefs. The symbolic storage area within the human brain for limiting subconscious beliefs and painful memories. Books symbolize beliefs and memories.

love. Energy at the highest and most creative vibration. Love is opposite in vibration to fear because it is unifying where fear is separating. *See also* undiluted love.

magenta singing light. The energies of the third-eye chakra (intuition) mixed with the root chakra (receiving). Visualizing the magenta energy supports the receiving of creative ideas from Soul. It also helps connect with the Divine Mothers (Goddesses) in Heaven.

magical. That which is miraculous, divinely inspired, and joyfully unexpected.

masculine brain. The logical, rational, and analytical part of your mind where the ego lives. The divine masculine of Soul raises the vibration of the male brain to help with focus and positivity. Fear's old male and old female attack through the masculine (ego) brain.

money. Currency in any form, including digital and plastic, that originates from the thoughtform of money. The thoughtform of money is made of fear; however, it can be raised in vibration. Money can play the role of an important teacher on Schoolroom Earth.

Mother of the Great Universe. Emotion, or sound, at the vibration of undiluted love. The highest vibrational receiving. The Divine

Mother's energy gives the ease of receiving from Source, emotional security, acceptance and approval, and physical safety.

Mother-Father-God. Synonymous with Source, Creator, Central Sun, Central Soul, and Divine Oneness. The "Mother" in Mother-Father-God is the Divine Mother, or Feminine, of the Great Universe. The "Father" in Mother-Father-God is the Divine Father, or Masculine, of the Great Universe.

nature Angel. The Angel that holds Creator's particles of energy in the form of a human being. The nature Angel is part of Soul.

One Human Body. Humanity. The human collective in which you are a cell. As you forgive and receive in wealth from the Great Universe, you help all cells in the One Human Body do the same.

patriarchal hierarchy. A structure of governance where fear's old male is the leader and fear's old female influences the minds of the followers.

personality. The Heart expression of any Soul. Angels and Ascended Masters have personalities. Any human personality that chooses fear is called an ego.

Power. Mother-Father-God's energy of undiluted love used to benefit Divine Oneness. The highest vibrational Power obeys the divine laws.

prosperity. The plentiful flow of financial resources in ways that do not require sacrifice of one's creative passions or mental, emotional, and physical health.

purple door. The gateway between the masculine logical brain and the feminine creative-intuitive brain. The purple door is made of the energy of the crown and third-eye chakras and cannot be contaminated by fear.

ray. Energy being emitted from the Central Sun in a color and with sound. *See also* singing light.

religion. Any belief system where separation between human and Creator/Source are part of the instruction, philosophy, or practice. When the religion has rules that give men power and privilege over others, fear and suffering will prevail.

ruby singing light. Divine Mother's energy of the root chakra that when visualized fills the human vessel with unconditional love, emotional security, and physical safety. This singing light is essential to receiving from the Great Universe.

sapphire blue or cobalt singing light. The energy of the Will (or throat) chakra that expresses courage, Truth, and justice. *See also* Archangel Michael.

singing light. A ray of the Central Sun. Sound and Light at the vibration of undiluted love. *See also* chakra; ray.

sisters of intuition and creativity. Symbolic of the clear intuition and creative genius that flow from Source and Soul into the feminine-receptive mind. Daughters of the Divine Mother of the Great Universe.

Soul. A drop of the Central Sun made of undiluted love that lives within Divine Oneness.

subconscious. The subconscious works like the astral filter by absorbing negative memories, thoughts, and emotions of the past. It stores fear and unforgiven experiences until they are cleared with love.

superconscious. The consciousness of Creator/Mother-Father-God/ Divine Oneness at the vibration of undiluted love, pure thought, and emotion.

surrender. The act of the ego letting go of control and expectations and trusting that Soul is in charge.

telepath. A being that can communicate with another being through thought. Telepathic beings sense and absorb the thoughts of others. Angels use telepathy to communicate.

thoughtform. Anything that has materialized on the mundane (Earth) plane or astral filter from thought energy. Because fear separates thought from emotion, thoughtforms have some contamination from fear. Manifestations from Creator are creations, not thoughtforms as described in this text.

treasure. The vast wealth of gifts, talents, abilities, and wisdom available to all Souls. Soul opens the treasure chest to the ego as the ego aligns with Heart.

Trust energy. The profound healing energy of Creator's Heart that fuses the ego and Soul together at the vibration of unconditional love. Trust energy is grounding, healing, and protective.

Truth. The highest vibrational love expressed as the clear direction from Soul and Divine Oneness. The Will of Heart. Truth is a power of Mother-Father-God that liberates those trapped in the illusion of fear. This Power is accessed through the Will (throat) chakra and the color of the singing light is sapphire blue.

turquoise singing light. The energies of the Will and heart chakras fused together. This singing light supports freedom, success, and the manifestation of happy dreams. *See also* Archangel Metatron.

undiluted love. Love energy that does not have any vibrations of fear. Undiluted love is the energy of the Central Sun/Mother-Father-God/Creator/Divine Oneness/Great Universe.

unworthiness. The lie soaked in fear that gives the message, "Do not ask because you are not good enough to receive."

violet-fire dumpster. The release and transformation location for beliefs that are no longer needed or wanted.

violet-fire energy of transformation and forgiveness. The healing energy of the crown chakra that transforms the fear locked in the deep subconscious. Forgiveness, used as a Power of undiluted love, reaches the DNA to change ancestral family patterns of loss. Violet fire is the same as violet singing light.

vortex. For this text, a positive energy vortex is made of undiluted love energy moving from Heaven to Earth.

wealth. The ability to receive from Source all that you need to feel safe, healthy, free, and happy. Wealth is abundance that encompasses creative expression, fulfillment, balance, and Heart service that benefits Divine Oneness. True abundance includes financial prosperity that manifests while respecting the three divine laws.

white fire. The energy of the eighth chakra, located above the head. White fire is used to purify energy contaminated with fear. *See also* white-gold singing light.

white-gold singing light. The energy of the Central Sun and the Source of all the chakra energies and colors of singing light.

worthiness. The infinite worth of every human being to receive healing, transformation, liberation, and abundance from the Great Universe.

wounded child. The self or selves that hold on to the hurts and traumas of the past. The wounded child wants to protect you from more hurt and loss even if this is greatly restrictive.

wounded female-feminine. The subconscious selves holding tight to guilt, shame, and victimization experiences from the past. The wounded female selves can be ancestral or from past lives. *See also* fear's old female.

wounded male-masculine. The subconscious or conscious selves acting from a place of anger, fear, and humiliation. The wounded male is directed by fear's old male. *See also* fear's old male.

Index

abandonment, fear of, 62, 113
abundance, 15, 20, 25, 106–7
abuse
  of children, transforming, 178–85
  DNA scrub for clearing, 183–85
  feelings and behaviors associated
    with, 180–82
air pollution, transforming, 207–13
Angel Love Doctors, 162
Angel of Death, 162
As Above, So Below, As Within, So
    Without, 8–10, 61, 92, 115, 145,
    165, 167, 195
auto loans/leases, 121
awareness
  bringing back home to yourself,
    138–40
  of guilt, 95
  negative thoughts and emotions, 208
  tools leading to, 72–73
  of what you're drawing to you, 92–93

balancing energy, 167, 210
beliefs
  income, 128
  outgrown, 149

poverty, 170–72
  subconscious, 51–56
black box, 110, 112–13, 149

Central Sun, 2, 12, 18, 21–27, 42–43,
    95, 105, 133–34
chakras
  about, 21
  all, color fusion, 26–27
  colors, 21–22
  first, 24–25
  second, 24, 166
  third, 24
  fourth, 23
  fifth, 23
  fifth and fourth color fusion, 25–26
  sixth, 22–23
  seventh, 22
  eighth, 22, 110
  eighth and fifth color fusion, 25
childhood abuse/neglect,
    transforming, 178–85
chocolate, 186–88
colors, singing. *See also* chakras
  about, 20, 21–22
  fusion of all, 26

old male and, 37
six-step formula and, 138–40
community garden, 131, 133–35
creativity. *See also* intuition
  ego measurement of, 87
  feminine brain and, 76
  firing up, 83–88
  as flowing water, 84
  hearing from, 70
  as leap of faith, 83–84
  as miracle ingredient, 78
  priming the pump of, 84–85
  sustainable flow and, 127–35
  wealth and, 74
creativity garden
  about, 77–78
  clearing weeds of doubt and fear
    from, 88
  community, 131, 133–35
  ego perspective, 84
  germination, 80–81
  harvesting, 98–102, 131–32
  patience and, 80–81
  planting, 79
  playing in, 82–83
  practices, 78–83
  supporting growth of, 83–88
credit card debt, 121
currency, 111, 204
currency trees, 233–34

discrimination, transforming,
  189–92
divine feminine, 18–19, 29–30, 38, 41,
  87, 98, 121, 145, 156, 209, 212–13
divine inner child
  about, 18–19
  acknowledging, 42

asking for something fun and
  nurturing, 81–82
checking in with, 69
as fearless, 42
gratitude and acknowledgment
  for, 29
healing and, 41–44, 215
listening to, 78–79
love relationships and, 145
as trustworthy messenger, 19
voice and appearance of,
  41–42
wealth practice, 19–20
wealthy life and, 145
divine laws
  about, 7
  As Above, So Below, As Within,
    So Without, 8–10, 61, 92, 115,
    145, 165, 167, 195
  ego and consciousness as
    expression, 7–8
  Law of Energy, 12–15
  Law of One, 10–12, 75, 90,
    105–6, 148, 167
  money and, 104–9
  religions and, 148
divine masculine, 18–19, 38, 78,
  87, 98, 121, 128, 197
Divine Oneness
  about, 10–11
  asking to receive love from, 14
  freedom and, 148
  grounding yourself in, 190
  lack of trust in, 106
  Law of One and, 11
  needed money and, 99–100
doing, constant, 207
doubt, conquering, 118–20

ego
  about, 7–8
  best income and, 128
  control and, 98
  false knowledge of, 60
  gratification and, 99–100, 193
  healing separation between Soul
    and, 42–43
  love relationships and, 143–44
  manifesting resources and, 35
  measuring creativity and, 87
  merging with needs of humanness,
    60–61
  rescuing, 100–101
  self-worth and, 153–54
  Soul(s) and, 154–56
  trust and, 156
  at vibration of divine love, 36
eighth chakra, 22, 25, 110
emotional and physical health, 158–63
emotions, 8–9, 12, 35–36, 155, 158–60,
    207–8, 210–11
energy, 12–13, 30, 192
evil, transforming, 186–88
exile, transforming, 175–77

fantasy scenarios, 73–75
fear(s)
  of abandonment, 62, 113, 175
  desire to shift in vibration, 12
  homelessness and exile, 174, 175–77
  love and, 5
  money and, 111, 126
  of natural resources running out,
    207
  old male/old female and, 36–37, 38–39
  puppet strings, 112–14
  of rejection, 101

from religion/government, 151–52
  religious doctrines and, 46
  shifting mind vibration out of, 4
  subconscious and, 3, 45, 55–56
  survival-based, 50–51
  transformation of, 141, 214–15
  vibrations of, 14
feminine brain, 29–30, 75, 76, 203
fifth chakra, 23, 25–26
financial debt
  about, 114–15, 116–17
  auto loans/leases and, 121
  credit cards and, 121
  dissolving, 116–26
  family patterns, transforming, 124–25
  mortgages and, 120–21
  as outer manifestation, 117
  shortchanged by the Creator, 117–18
  short-term personal loans and, 123–24
  subconscious and symbolic
    messages of, 116
  symbolic meaning of, 120–23
  taxes and, 120
financial trauma/suffering, clearing,
    106–8
first chakra, 24–25
focus, switching, 95
forgiveness
  debts and, 116
  Heart Power and, 93
  learning to practice, 45
  love relationships and, 144
  parents and, 179
  of the past, 146–47
  practicing, 45, 50
  of that which is unforgivable, 179, 180
  traumas of childhood, 182–83
four-pointed cross, 150

fourth chakra, 23, 25–26
freedom, 147, 148–52

Gabriel, Archangel, xiv, 25, 107, 119.
    See also specific Archangels
Gaia, Archangel, 2, 12, 25, 161,
    189–92, 212
garden. *See* creativity garden
grace, 141, 144, 156, 174
gratitude
    As Above, So Below, As Within, So
        Without and, 89
    for Divine Mother, 29
    Heart Power and, 94
    for a safe home, 176
    as super vibration shifter, 176
    thinking thoughts of, 12
    trust and, 120
    for your own value, 139
guilt, 65–66, 95

happy receiving, support of, 217–36
harvesting your garden, 98–102
hatred, transforming, 186–88
healing
    divine inner child, 215
    planetary, 11
    receiving, 43–44
    separation between ego and Soul,
        42–43
    supporting, 218
    undiluted love, 159
    visualizations and, 5
    wounded self, 50
Healing Experiences
    Activating Heart Power, 96–97
    Bringing Peace and Balance to
        Earth, 165–66

Clearing Financial Trauma and
    Suffering, 107–8
Clearing Repression of the
    Feminine, 76–77
Clearing the Pipeline, 131
Conquering Doubt, 118–20
Credit and Validation for You, 122–23
Deep Cleansing for Old Male and
    Old Female, 205–6
Divine Mothers' Palace of Renewal, 221
Divine Rescue, 187–88
DNA Scrub for Clearing Neglect
    and Abuse, 183–85
Doubt Out, Trust In, 67
Dragon's Roost with the Divine
    Inner Child, 220
Emerald and Ruby in a Golden
    Nest Egg, 227
Emerald Forest, 231
Entering the Sanctuary of Soul, 156–57
Filling Up with All You Could
    Ever Want, 63
Firing Up Your Creativity, 85–87
Forgiving the Past, 146–47
Forgiving the Traumas of
    Childhood, 182–83
Freedom Within, Freedom
    Without, 64–65
Freeing the Repressed Masculine,
    80–81
Golden Pyramid of Initiation with
    the 12 Archangels, 235–36
Goodbye Negativity and Good
    Night!, 219
Graceful Exit from the Dance Floor, 162
Gratitude for You, 230
Healing Session with the Angel
    Physicians, 161

Healing the Divine Inner Child, 215
Healing the Wounded Self, 50
Into the Purple Sea, 225
Letting Go of Fear's Old Female
   Poverty Beliefs, 171–72
Letting Go of the Magic Parent, 75
Love Alarm, 39–40
Merlin's Cabin and Cocoa, 223
Mother Earth's Haven, 228
New Beginning, A, 15–16
Orchard of Ever-Growing Currency
   Trees, 233–34
Planting Your Creativity Garden, 79
Playing in the Garden of Your
   Creative Imagination, 82–83
Rainbow Embrace, 26–27
Rebalancing the Power of the
   Divine Feminine, 212–13
Receive, Attract, Focus, and Grow!,
   132–33
Receiving Guidance and Healing,
   43–44
Receiving the Invitation, 5–6
Reclaiming Your Highest
   Vibrational Will, 195–96
Releasing Ancestral and Past-Life
   Trauma, 58
Releasing the Expectation of Being
   Abandoned by Creator, 62
Releasing the Negative Parent
   Voice, 71–72
Releasing the Puppet Strings of
   Attachment to Money, 114
Rescuing the Ego, 100–101
Restoring in the Energy Fountains,
   32–34
Stepping through the Purple Door,
   30–31

to support sleep and happy
   receiving, 217–36
Surfing with the 12 Archangels, 222
Transforming Family Patterns of
   Debt, 124–25
Transforming Fear Caused by
   Religion and Government, 151–52
Transforming or Eliminating
   Conflict from Inside Out, 201–2
Transforming Poverty from the
   Inside Out, 172–74
Transforming Subconscious
   Unworthiness and Guilt, 47
Transforming Your Heartache, 91–92
Transmuting Lack Beliefs, 56–58
Transmuting the Judges, 191–92
Undiluted Love for You, 65–66
Violet Fire for Releasing the
   Trauma of Exile, 176–77
Working with the Young
   Masculine, 199–202
health, 158–63
health concerns, 159–60
Heart, the
   creativity garden and, 77
   feminine brain and, 30
   negative potential of exile and, 175
   trust between wounded self and, 49
   trust in Source and, 46
heart chakra, 31–32
Heart Power
   activating, 96–97, 140
   attraction, 90–91, 126
   awareness of what you're drawing to
      you and, 92–93
   community garden and, 134
   creativity and, 88
   cultivating, 3, 89–97

daily tools for activation and
   expansion, 92–97
divine inner child and, 42
ego pressure and, 95
forgiveness and, 93
gratitude, 94
guilt awareness and, 95
human interaction and, 90–91
lacking, 94–95
mindfulness of religious beliefs
   and, 94–95
self-acceptance and, 94
switching focus and, 95
third divine law and, 90
young masculine acting from, 198
Heaven, as healing sanctuary, 31–32
Helpers in Heaven, 19–20, 70, 105,
   127, 154, 162
homelessness, transforming, 175–77

"I am not enough," 53–55
inequality, transforming, 189–92, 203–4
intuition, 29, 37, 69, 70. *See also*
   creativity

lack
   beliefs, transmuting, 56–58
   repetitive story of, 45–58
   as subconscious belief, 51–56
Law of Energy, 12–15, 210
Law of One, 10–12, 75, 90, 105–6,
   148, 167
leadership, transforming, 193–96
letting go, 76, 154
living your purpose, 155
love
   about, 2
   as alchemical power, 2

asking to receive, 14
dissolving financial debt with, 116–26
divine inner child and, 18–19
fear and, 5
health and, 159
money and, 111
power of, money and, 109
Soul and, 144
transforming fear into, 214–15
transforming hatred, violence, and
   evil with, 186–88
unconditional, 141
love relationships, 143–47

magic parent, 72–75, 122
Meet Your Guardian Angels
   workshop, xiii–xiv
Michael, Archangel, xiv, 23, 43, 80,
   108, 119, 171, 180, 187
money
   attachment, puppet strings, 112–14
   black box, 110, 112–13, 149
   changing "hands" of, 104
   currency and, 111, 204
   divine laws and, 104–9
   fear and, 111, 126
   frequency of, 109
   hoarding, 106
   love and, 111
   power of love and, 109
   reality, changing, 109
   sharing, 105–6
   vibration and, 13
mortgages, 120–21
Mother Earth, 210

natural resource exploitation,
   transforming, 207–13

nature, 68–69

negative parent prison, 70–73

old female archetype, 38–39, 51, 69, 113, 194, 204–6

old male archetype, 39, 67, 69, 113, 204–6, 208

One Human Body
  about, 3
  balance within, 167
  cell communication within, 167
  healing Earth and, 208
  helping awaken, 204
  subconscious, 4, 9
  suffering, changing, 4–5

pain, childhood, 179

parent(s), 70–73, 179. *See also* magic parent

patriarchal hierarchy, transforming, 203–6

peace and balance, 164–68

pipeline, clearing, 131

pipeline blockers, 128–30

poverty, transforming, 170–74

power misuse, transforming, 193–96

pressure, 95, 155

puppet strings, 112–14

purple door, the, 28–31

racism, transforming, 189–92

rainbow bridge, 162, 189

Receiving the Invitation, 5–6

religion
  beliefs, 94–95
  divine laws and, 148
  doctrines, 46
  fear caused by, 151–52

safety/security need, 61–62

second chakra, 24, 166

self-acceptance, 94

seventh chakra, 22

six-step formula, 138–40

sixth chakra, 22–23

sleep, support of, 217–36

Soul(s)
  about, 2–3
  asking for what is missing, xv
  Central Soul and, 9–10
  creative genius, 87
  desires, receiving, 138–40
  ego and, 7, 154–56
  healing separation between ego and, 42–43
  intelligence of, 9
  lack of trust in, 106
  as leaves, 192
  living the mission of, 153–57
  love and, 144
  as one, 9–10
  pain from childhood and, 179
  receiving assistance from, 70
  recognition, 4
  sanctuary, entering, 156–57
  support of, 66
  surrender to, 69, 78–79, 195

spiritual service, 111

subconscious beliefs
  asking for as forbidden and hopeless and, 52
  beginning of lack as, 51–56
  experience examples, 55
  fears and, 55–56
  list of, 52, 53–55
  survival-based fears, 50–51
  transmuting, 56–58

subconscious motivations
  guilt, 65–66
  influencing what you believe you
    want, 61–67
  need for freedom, 64
  need for safety/security, 61–62
  need to be wanted and valued, 63
surrender, 15, 28, 41, 69, 78–79, 100,
  194–95
survival-based fears, 50–51
sustainable flow, creativity and, 127–35

taxes, 120
third chakra, 24
time and money, 13–14
transformation
  Central Sun and, 42–43
  exile and homelessness, 175–77
  family patterns of debt, 124–25
  fear, 141, 214–15
  hatred, violence, and evil, 186–88
  heartache, 91–92
  inequality, racism, and
    discrimination, 189–92
  leadership and the misuse of power,
    193–96
  neglect and abuse of children, 178–85
  patriarchal hierarchy, 203–6
  pollution and exploitation of
    natural resources, 207–13
  poverty, 170–74
  religious fear, 151–52
  survival-based beliefs, 50–51
  unworthiness and guilt, 47–48
  warfare and military action, 197–202
trauma, 11, 49, 51, 58, 64, 106–8,
  182–83

triggers, awareness of, 69–70
trust
  calling into mind and body, 66–67
  Divine Oneness and, 100
  ego and consciousness as expression,
    156
  energy of, 68
  gratitude and, 120
  healing, 50
  in Source, xiv–xv, 45
  between wounded self and the
    Heart, 49
Truth
  disconnection and, 178
  glossary of terms to feel, xv–xvi
  love and, 19
  recognizing messages of, 41
  spine symbolism, 150
12 Archangels, xiii–xvi, 39, 78–83,
  138–41. *See also specific Archangels*

Victoria, Archangel, 23, 151, 171, 180
violence, transforming, 186–88
visualizations, 5, 56, 140

warfare/military action, transforming,
  197–202
wealth
  creativity and, 74
  definition of, 18–20
  divine inner child practice, 19–20
  events that express emotions,
    210–11
  what does it look like? 60–67
wounded self, befriending, 48–50

young masculine, 197–202